FANON

and the
Crisis of
European Man

FANON

and the
Crisis of
European Man

An Essay on Philosophy
and the Human Sciences

LEWIS R. GORDON

ROUTLEDGE
New York and London

Published in 1995 by

Routledge
270 Madison Ave,
New York NY 10016

Published in Great Britain in 1995 by

Routledge
2 Park Square, Milton Park,
Abingdon, Oxon, OX14 4RN

Transferred to Digital Printing 2008

Copyright © 1995 by Routledge

Library of Congress Cataloging-in-Publications Data

Gordon, Lewis R. (Lewis Ricardo)
    Fanon and the crisis of European man : an essay on philosophy and the human sciences
/ Lewis R. Gordon
    p. cm.
    Includes bibliographical references and index.
    ISBN 0-415-91414- 0 — ISBN 0-415-91415-9
    1. Fanon, Frantz, 1925-1961. 2. Phenomenology. 3. Existentialism. 4. Europe—Civilization—
20th century. 5. Social sciences—Philosophy. I. Title.
    B1029.F354G67 1995
    325' .3' 092—dc20   95-8756
                                                                                              CIP

Publisher's Note
The publisher has gone to great lengths to ensure the quality of this reprint but points out
that some imperfections in the original may be apparent

In Memory of

Frantz Fanon
1925–1961

Patrice Lamumba
1925–1961

El-Haji Malik El-Shabazz
1925–1965

Robert Blair
1964–1994

Contents

Preface and Acknowledgments

ix

Introduction

1

ONE

Fanon as Critique of European Man

5

TWO

Existential Phenomenology and History

13

THREE

Racism, Colonialism, and Anonymity:
Social Theory and Embodied Agency

37

FOUR

Tragic Revolutionary Violence and Philosophical Anthropology

67

FIVE

Fanon's Continued Relevance

85

Notes

105

Bibliography

117

Index

129

Preface and
Acknowledgments

THIS BOOK was presented by the author at a number of conferences during the spring of 1994. The idea of writing this work on Frantz Fanon, one of the most influential philosophers, psychiatrists, sociologists, and revolutionaries of the twentieth century, grew out of an important conference and three pivotal conversations over the past two years. The conference was the Sixth Biennial Meeting of the Sartre Society of North America, held at Trent University in Peterborough, Ontario. At the conference, I presented a paper that aroused interest in my discussion of Fanon's relationship to Jean-Paul Sartre. Some of those ideas were later included in my essay, "Sartrean Bad Faith and Antiblack Racism," published in *The Prism of the Self: Essays in Honor of Maurice Natanson*.[1] An excerpt from that essay appears in the second chapter of this work by permission of Kluwer Academic Publishers.

The first conversation that influenced my decision to write this book preceded the conference, however, by half a year. It was with my colleague and friend, Paget Henry, with whom I have been in

correspondence ever since I presented a paper on bad faith and
antiblack racism at the Center for the Study of Race and Ethnicity at
Brown University during the fall semester of 1992. We have shared
work since then and have spoken quite a bit about Fanon. Out of
those conversations emerged a special section on Fanon in my first
book, *Bad Faith and Antiblack Racism*.[2]

The second pivotal conversation came out of a correspondence
with Bob Stone of Long Island University, who reviewed my first book
for publication. His commentary raised some challenges regarding my
interpretation of Fanon's work. Through our correspondence, he
became persuaded by my positions on Fanon and phenomenology and
encouraged me to produce a work on those themes.

The third experience was with my colleague, Martin Matuštík,
whose work, *Postnational Identity*, marks a recent effort to forge a place
for the convergence of existential philosophy and critical theory.[3] We
had decided to present works on two central figures in the "New
Left"—I on Fanon, and Martin on Herbert Marcuse. But as we met and
sat down to compose our papers, we each came to the realization that
we had much more to say than we had bargained for at that time; for
such convergences are intimately linked to our philosophical projects,
which involve the articulation and defense of a place for the human
being in misanthropic times. The consequence was our "going with the
pitch," and, in my case, developing presentations toward a work in celebration of Fanon's seventieth birthday. To this end, I have benefitted
from the kindness of a number of individuals and institutions.

Leonard Harris has provided me with opportunities and resources
in the presentation of various sections of this book. Early versions of
the first and second chapters were presented at the Cultural Studies
Collective at Purdue University, the Black Caucus's symposium,
Existential Perspectives on Nationality, Race, and Resistance, which was held
at the American Philosophical Association–Pacific Division meeting,
and the Critical Theory Conference on Democracy and Identity,
which was held at the Czech Academy of Science. With regard to these
conferences, I would like to thank Grant Snider for the Purdue gig,

Leonard Harris and Tommy Lott for the Los Angeles one, as well as my wonderful friend, Mina Choi, for the great time and support in L.A., and, finally, the Purdue Research Foundation for the much-needed funds to travel to Prague. In Prague, Josef Moural of Charles University proved to be a helpful guide and a source of stimulating conversation on phenomenology.

I should also like to note two unexpected circumstances that emerged out of the L.A. and Prague conferences. Antole Anton, who chaired the panel discussion in L.A., wrote a rather interesting editorial to the *Proceedings and Addresses of the American Philosophical Association*, in which he remarked that "if not explicitly critiquing 'constitutionalism,' the panelists (which included Matuštík and Ronald Judy) in the Symposium on Existentialist Perspectives on Race and Nationality were, at least, firmly grounded in the twentieth century."[4] He identified a key dimension of my project when he added: "In one way or another, they were all reflecting on the meaning of the practical failures of the liberal state to live up to its own ideals. 'To what extent,' they all seemed to ask in different ways, 'are liberal categories obsolete?'" I thank Anton both for chairing the panel and for restating these important questions.

I would like to add how I became acquainted with a wonderful group of Czech philosophers at Charles University. At the main conference held at the Czech Academy of Science, there were dynamics that struck me as indicative of the crisis that will be discussed in subsequent chapters. I presented this work during what has become known in the critical theory circle as the infamous "second week," the week reserved for the younger scholars. Most of the older, élite scholars took it upon themselves to depart after their presentations during the first week. In both weeks, only one Czech philosopher participated. Since my philosophical inclinations are more rooted in existential phenomenology and liberation theory, I went to my Czech colleague Martin Matuštík's book session at Charles University. That session and our ensuing long conversations on philosophy and politics proved to be the most memorable intellectual dimension of my visit to Prague.

The third chapter, and elements of the fourth, were presented at the Sixth Annual Conference of North American and Cuban Philosophers and Social Scientists in Havana, Cuba. I would like to thank Joy James for inviting me to present my work in front of such a committed and interesting group of scholars. Joy has been, and continues to be, a source of intellectual and spiritual strength. She is a people's philosopher with whom I'm sure Fanon would have had much to discuss. I would also like to thank Eduardo Lorenzo for his assistance in presenting my work to the Cuban scholars at that conference, as well as Warren Crichlow for roommate and beach-side discussions on the third and fourth chapters.

I have also benefitted from ongoing discussion and encouragement of my project on Fanon from the following colleagues at Purdue University: William McBride, Calvin Schrag, Floyd Hayes, III, Edith Clowes, Patricia Morris, Bernice Carol (who invited me to discuss Fanon in her class on international politics), Vernon Williams, T. Denean Sharpley-Whiting (who read and commented on the manuscript), and my students, Peter Okeafor, Daphne Thompson, Fred Santiago Arroyo, Hardie Davidson, Matthew Barnes, and Michele O'Brien. I would also like to thank the secretaries of the Philosophy Department, Pam Connely, Elizabeth Smith, and Bonnie Memmering, and in the African American Studies program, Christina Boyd and Edna Fox, for clerical assistance at various stages of this project. And in terms of ongoing discussion and encouragement of my work, my colleague, neighbor, and friend, Gloria Soto, who read and commented on an early version of this entire manuscript, deserves special thanks.

I would like to thank my friend, Mohammedyazid Bendjeddou in Algeria, for the times we've shared discussing political, literary, and philosophical matters. Unfortunate circumstances brought him back to Algeria before the completion of his research project at Purdue. I hope things take a turn for the better and I would like you to know, Mohammed, that your words of encouragement were well appreciated and I will always cherish our times together.

Thanks are also due to Maurice Natanson, M. Shawn Copeland, and Cora Monroe for their continued support, especially through some rough times that emerged during the course of writing this work, and Gary Schwartz, whose friendship is such that he can indulge a discussion on translating Aristotle's *Poetics* over long-distance telephone on a rainy Friday evening, as well as a late-Monday-night discussion on various sections of Rousseau's *Emile*. Nigel Gibson also deserves a note of appreciation for a last-minute citation via e-mail.

And of course, there are Lisa, Mathieu, and Jennifer Gordon, Renée White, Pat Garel, Sylvia Crosdale, Gertrude Stoddart, Mark and Robert Evans, Maurice Gordon, and my extended family, especially my Aunt Lola Blair. Without these people, my efforts (philosophical, political and academic), would lack a great deal of personal meaning.

Finally, Robert Blair, whose name appears in the dedication, died from illness that emerged as a consequence of AIDS. He was my cousin whom I loved and with whom I have shared many fond memories. I was not aware that the last time I held him in my arms was truly goodbye. I hope this is a book of which he would have been proud.

L.R.G.
West Lafayette, Indiana
February 1995

Introduction

FRANTZ FANON was born on the island of Martinique. He died on the 6th of December, 1961, of bronchial pneumonia, apparently as a consequence of leukemia. He died in Bethesda, Maryland, where he was brought at great resistance for treatment of his illness upon the recommendation of physicians in the former Soviet Union. The Algerian war of liberation against French colonialism was at its most fierce as it was coming to a close. Fanon was a key figure in the Algerian FLN (National Liberation Front). Before he died, he declared that he would have preferred to have been sent back to the Algerian battlefield, where even with his frail, sickly body he could have been thrown as a strike against the enemy's dehumanization of humankind, instead of being left to rot in a place that he regarded as "the nation of lynchers." His corpse was flown back to Algeria, where it was laid to rest in a shallow grave on the Algerian battlefield. On the 20th of June 1995, he would have been seventy.

Emmanuel Hansen observes:

Fanon was not exclusively a man of study: he was also a man of action. He tried to live his ideas and act in such a way as to bring the ideas in which he believed into being. In this way, his life and personality were inextricably linked with his ideas.[1]

Hansen identifies four perspectives from which Fanon can be examined: political philosophy, social science, ideology, and myth-making. He adds, "It is my view that, in order to gain a clear understanding of the totality and complexity of Fanon's thought, his work must be viewed from all of the above perspectives, and that is the approach taken in this study."

I would add two other perspectives: the perspective of philosophical anthropology and the perspective of the philosophy of the human sciences. It is in the effort to develop his relevance to these fifth and sixth perspectives, perspectives whose twentieth-century points of origin are crises of what G. W. F. Hegel predicted to be stages of self-consciousness, that I have conducted this study. Like Hansen, it is also my view that the other four must be kept present so as to bring out the complexity of Fanon's ideas.

This study is not a study *on* Fanon so much as it is an opportunity for an engagement *with* Fanon. There have been plenty of the first kind of study—some good, many bad. I'm sure there will be more. Instead, I here regard Fanon as a locus of many pressing questions in contemporary philosophy—particularly in philosophy of human science. Regarding Fanon as an opportunity, I regard myself as working within the spirit of his way of seeing the world, since, like Edmund Husserl, Fanon respected most those who have the courage to state what they believe. I believe Fanon was a great philosopher and that his ideas continue to be of great value to other philosophers, cultural critics, human scientists, and laypeople alike.

In this regard, it should be noted that these concerns place this study in a different focus than Hussein Abdilahi Bulhan's *Frantz Fanon and the Psychology of Oppression*,[2] a text which I regard to be among the very best studies on Fanon. Bulhan's focus is on a specific dimension of the human sciences—namely psychology—and throughout, he issues a critique of Euro-science that is premised more upon *European scientists* than the question of whether science itself can avoid being European.

Fanon did believe that science itself can avoid being European. Ultimately, he believed so because European science has been much like the history of television. Its producers continue to believe that they bring us the world because they have defined the world so narrowly.

ONE

Fanon as Critique
of European Man

Leave us alone without any books, and we shall at once get confused, lose ourselves in a maze, we shall not know what to cling to, what to hold on to, what to love and what to hate, what to respect and what to despise. We even find it hard to be men, men of *real* flesh and blood, *our own* flesh and blood. We are ashamed of it. We think it a disgrace. And we do our best to be some theoretical "average" men.
                                    —Fyodor Dostoyevsky, *Notes from Underground*

They approach me in a half-hesitant sort of way, eye me curiously or compassionately, and then, instead of saying directly, How does it feel to be a problem? they say, I know an excellent colored man in my town; or, I fought at Mechanicsville; or, Do not these Southern outrages make your blood boil? At these I smile, or am interested, or reduce the boiling to a simmer, as the occasion may require. To the real question, How does it feel to be a problem? I answer seldom a word.
                                    —W.E.B. Du Bois, *The Souls of Black Folk*

[W]hen the white American, holding up most twentieth-century fiction, says, "This is American reality," the Negro tends to answer (not at all concerned that Americans tend generally to fight against any but the most flattering imaginative depictions of their lives), "Perhaps, but you've left out this, and this, and this. And most of all, what you'd have the world accept as *me* isn't even human."
                                    —Ralph Ellison, *Shadow and Act*

"Dirty nigger!" or simply, "Look, a Negro!"
                                    —Frantz Fanon, *Black Skin, White Masks*

F RANTZ FANON, the Frantz Fanon we encounter in writings on colonialism, neocolonialism, and racism, is a Frenchman and not a Frenchman.[1] This is because Frantz Fanon is black. He simultaneously *is* and *is not* in a peculiar way. He is too much. And he is not enough. He is, as he says, echoing Sartre's expression from *Anti-Semite and Jew*, "overdetermined from without." As it goes with such a situation, or perhaps "condition," to be black means to face the fact of being *too* black. He is not white enough, which means that he is not human enough. In his situation, Fanon does not live as a criticism of France, and consequently of Europe. For to live as such is to live from the standpoint of the possibility of alteriorizing and de-centering France. But France is not Fanon's Other; he is *France's* Other. Like the African American, Fanon finds himself inextricably linked to a society that not only rejects him, but also attempts to deny his existence as a legitimate point of view, in some cases—as in its current postmodern-poststructural excursions—denying the very theoretical assumptions from which he may even demand his day in the tribunal of human affairs. He lives as a critique of France. He embodies its critique. From Fanon's experience, which he claims ultimately counts as an extension of a manifold experience that constitutes the experience of the oppressed, we learn that the twentieth-century person of color embodies a crisis of Europe and Euro-reason.[2]

By Europe, we mean Edmund Husserl's description of a place that is "not as it is understood geographically, as on a map, as if thereby the group of people who live together in this territory would define European humanity. In the spiritual sense, the English Dominions, the United States, etc., clearly belong to Europe. . . . Here the title 'Europe' clearly refers to the unity of a spiritual life, activity, creation, with all its ends, interests, cares, and endeavors, with its products of purposeful activity, institutions, organizations."[3]

There is a taste of irony and a tone of desperation in Husserl's delineation of European humanity, for it is clear that by the time of his *Crisis of European Sciences*—his sermon on European Reason—that

6

there were not only Europe*s*, but also a simultaneously ghostly Europe. Although Europe was condemned to a splintered existence, it was simultaneously exhibiting a form of vibrancy that made it all too clear that Husserl, though correctly delineating Europe, was not seeing Europe from the point of view from which it actually "lived." Resuscitation became the order of the day, and in the effort at such rebirth came the effort to reconstitute a world which was, as Richard Rorty later declares, "well lost." We encounter Husserlian crisis immediately, then, as not only a crisis of meaning, but also a crisis of valuative malaise or, as Jürgen Habermas later declares, a problem of legitimation on every level of social life.[4] In Husserl's hands, this crisis is identified in clinical form. "The European nations are sick; Europe itself, it is said, is in crisis. We are by no means lacking something like nature doctors. Indeed, we are practically inundated by a flood of naïve and excessive suggestions for reform. But why do the so richly developed humanistic disciplines fail to perform the service here that is so admirably performed by the natural sciences in their sphere?" (*Crisis*, p. 270). Husserl's complaint is that practitioners of the human sciences, philosophy, and cultural criticism often identify the symptoms, but they shrink cowardly from the task involved in identifying the disease.

Let us return to Fanon's diagnosis. If the twentieth-century person of color symbolizes a crisis of European Man, to what extent is his embodiment of this crisis a clue to an identification of the disease? Fanon confesses his existential encounter with this dimension of the crisis itself:

> The psychoanalysts say that nothing is more traumatizing for the young child than his encounters with what is rational. I would personally say that for a man whose only weapon is reason there is nothing more neurotic than contact with unreason. I felt knife blades open within me. I resolved to defend myself. As a good tactician, I intended to rationalize the world and to show the white man that he was mistaken. . . . Reason was confident of victory on every level. I put all the parts back together. But I had to change my tune. That victory played cat and mouse; it made a fool of me. As the other put it, when I was present, it was not; when it was there, I was no longer. (*Black Skin, White Masks*, pp. 118–120)

7

Fanon's existence raises the question of the relationship between humanity and reason, and problems raised by what he calls "the fact of blackness." If even reason or the understanding is infected with racism, where unreason stands on the opposite pole as a Manichaean abyss of blackness, then a black man who reasons finds himself in the absurdity of the very construction of himself as a black man *who reasons,* much like the confused apprehension of "white civilization and dignity" (p. 63) felt when a black man's hands caress a white woman's breast.[5] He faces humanity as a Sartrean *for-itself* faces its ego. He seeks himself "here," but forever encounters himself—"there." Whereas for Husserl there was a nightmare of disintegrated reason, for Fanon there was the nightmare of racist reason itself—reason that leaves him out in the cold.

Friedrich Nietzsche once announced that not only was God dead, but also that European man was sick.[6] We already see that, as an indictment on the twentieth century, Husserl concurs. Fanon, the man of color, smirks. Why sound the alarm for the discovery of a fool? Why worry about *that* sickness?

> The colonialist bourgeoisie, in its narcissistic dialogue, expounded by the members of its universities, had in fact deeply implanted in the minds of the colonized intellectual that the essential qualities remain eternal in spite of all the blunders men may make: the essential qualities of the West, of course. The native intellectual accepted the cogency of these ideas, and deep down in his brain you could always find a vigilant sentinel ready to defend the Greco-Latin pedestal. Now it so happens that during the struggle for liberation, at the moment that the native intellectual comes into touch again with his people, this artificial sentinel is turned into dust. All the Mediterranean values—the triumph of the human individual, of clarity, and of beauty—become lifeless, colorless knickknacks. All those speeches seem like collections of dead words; those values which seemed to uplift the soul are revealed as worthless, simply because they have nothing to do with the concrete conflict in which the people is engaged.[7]

Humanity has died in Europe, the United States, and anywhere in the world in which Western Man—that is, White Man/White

Culture—*is* Man and, therefore, Reason. In other words, humanity has suffered a global death. But in Euro-man, ironically even in his "colored" manifestations, lives the fool precisely because he thinks he is morally and rationally alive. He has no pulse. But he walks. He seems to walk on air, since his solid foundations no longer lay beneath him.

Where is he?

For Fanon, he is unfortunately everywhere, blocking the possibility of another who Fanon hopes will one day break free from bondage:

> If we wish to reply to the expectations of the people of Europe, it is no good sending them back a reflection, even an ideal reflection, of their society and their thought with which from time to time they feel immeasurably sickened. (*The Wretched of the Earth*, p. 316)

So, Fanon has kept the faith from his early period in *Black Skin, White Masks*, where he writes:

> Mankind, I believe in you. . . . From all sides dozens and hundreds of pages assail me and try to impose their wills on me. But a single line would be enough. Supply a single answer and the color problem would be stripped of all its importance. What does a man want? What does the black man want? (pp. 7–8)

Fanon poses this question, the question of Man, the anthropological question, to remind all of us that one cannot legitimately study man without remembering that desires and values emanate from him and shake the contours of investigation. For Fanon, this amounts in one instance to the methodology of what he calls a "sociogenic" approach, an approach standing outside of phylogeny and ontogeny, an approach that involves the understanding that the problem and interpretation at hand must be addressed "on the objective level as on the subjective level" (p. 11). In another instance, Fanon's investigations amount to a rejection of ontology, the study of Being, *from* which, *of* which, and *in* which, it seems, the very notions of the objective and the subjective can make sense:

In the *Weltanschauung* of a colonized people there is an impurity, a flaw that outlaws any ontological explanation. Someone may object that this is the case with every individual, but such an objection merely conceals a basic problem. Ontology—*once it is finally admitted as leaving existence by the wayside*—does not permit us to understand the being of the black man. For not only must the black man be black; he must be black in relation to the white man. (emphasis added, pp. 109–110)

This is not to say that Fanon rejects the thesis, espoused by W.E.B. Du Bois, Almicar Cabral, and C.L.R. James, that there are cultural aspects of native and enslaved people that survive the onslaught of a conquering people. His point is that there is an impact on the colonized group that mars classical ontological descriptions. Fanon rejects traditional ontological dimensions of human beings in favor of existential ones. He reminds us that the thing that he is not is realized *as* him when he jerks. Shakes. Fears. Trembles. Desires. Resists. Fights.

Fanon demands a rigorous, positive critique of validity criteria and method in the study and liberating praxis of (or, at times, *from*) black existence. He wants a radical posing of the question of Man. One will be hard-pressed to find a more radical and ultimately frightening questioning of humanity than the life and writings of Frantz Fanon.[8]

Yet *his* questioning of the questioning of man isn't so radical that he ceases to see the world. He offers a sociogenesis that demands a coordination of dichotomous concerns. He throws himself into existence and draws himself back to scope out his surroundings.

Why?

Fanon rejects ontology, but he does not reject the existential phenomenological impact of what he "sees." This is because he is fundamentally a radical, critical, revolutionary, existential humanist. In his words:

The disaster of the man of color lies in the fact that he was enslaved. The disaster and the inhumanity of the white man lie in the fact that somewhere he has killed man. (p. 231)

Four years later, in his resignation letter from Blida-Joinville we find a similar verdict:

> Madness is one of the means man has of losing his freedom. . . . If psychiatry is the medical technique that aims to enable man no longer to be a stranger to his environment, I woe it to myself to affirm that the Arab, permanently an alien in his own country, lives in a state of absolute depersonalization. What is the status of Algeria? A systematized de-humanization.[9]

To live a human existence means to be estranged by racism. Affective adjustment under racist conditions—the "well-adjusted slave"—is an obscenity. That even the white man is expected to be well-adjusted in his role as the master in a racist society is also an obscenity. By 1961, Fanon had witnessed the outermost limits of the human ability to behave inhumanely through direct engagement in the horrors of the war for Algerian independence. He writes:

> Because it is a systematic negation of the other person and a furi- ous determination to deny the other person all attributes of human- ity, colonialism forces the people it dominates to ask themselves the question constantly: "In reality, who am I?" . . . In Algeria there is not simply the domination but the decision to the letter not to occupy anything more than the sum total of the land. The Algerians, the veiled women, the palm trees, and the camels make up the landscape, the *natural* background to the human presence of the French. (*The Wretched of the Earth*, p. 250)

Man needs a radical form of self-reflection. For whatever may be abstracted from him as contingent faces its own delusion of reality. "Man," "Person," "Self," "Individual," "Community," even "Other," have peculiar, racialized residues of "White Man," "White Person," "White Ego," "White Individual," and "White Community." Their "glow" permeates praxis and restricts anthropological possibilities. Fanon wants to find Man, but he keeps bumping into White Man, or perhaps more appropriately, White Men. In *Black Skin, White Masks*, he finds himself manacled beyond the ties of the Other. A white man experiences the Other, but in an antiblack world there is no black person's Other

11

except among blacks; over and against him, there is the governing fiction *cum* reality of the White Man, whose usurpation Fanon reminds us marks "The End of the World" (pp. 215–216). Fanon's "End" seems to be equally as ambiguous as the celebrated yet infamous postmodern "End of Philosophy" or "End of Man." For the white man looks at the black man and wonders when it will all end, but the white man knows deep down that a just future is one in which he himself no longer exists in virtue of his ceasing to function as the End, or less ambiguously, the telos of Man. European Man dreads, then, as Lenin once put it, what is to be done.

So, Fanon's humanism marks its path rather early: "To educate man to be *actional*, preserving in all his relations his respect for the basic values that constitute a human world, is the prime task of him who, having taken thought, prepares to act" (p. 222).

The dialectic is issued. There is no extra-practical realm frozen above time here. There is the call for engagement. Man is not understood, especially in the contemporary form of White Man, who, for Fanon, is anti-Man. Man needs to emerge out of the ashes of the fact of his desiccation. In Fanon's own words:

> For Europe, for ourselves, and for humanity, comrades, we must turn over a new leaf, we must work out new concepts, and try to set afoot a new man. (*The Wretched of the Earth*, p. 316)

In the true sense of *kreinein* ("to decide," from which evolved the word *crisis*), Fanon embodies the crisis of European man as decision, whether favorable or unfavorable: there is no guarantee either of the good or the bad in the new. Yet the existential reality is issued. Crisis is the hidden decision not to decide. A decision to decide demands the challenge of a new day.

TWO

Existential Phenomenology and History

Since its beginning, phenomenology has been attempting to solve a problem which is not the problem of a sect but, perhaps, the problem of our time. . . . The sciences of man (psychology, sociology, history) . . . found themselves in a crisis situation. To the extent that it was really advancing, research in these fields was tending to show that all opinion, and in particular all philosophy, was the result of external psychological, social, and historical conditions working in combination. . . . The crisis of science in general, of the sciences of man, and of philosophy leads to an irrationalism.

—Merleau-Ponty

Man does not, cannot, live in a valueless world.

—Alain Locke

FANON FACES a peculiar problem.[1] If ontology offers nothing for the understanding of the black man, then a scientific study of blacks would require a science that has no ontology. Ontology must thus be "suspended." Fanon, in effect, makes a phenomenological move. Yet, ironically, *existence* pulls him back into the problem of *not* being able to "bracket" ontology. Fanon faces a number of problems from many angles—all of which relate to the problem of radicalizing the study of human being.

In his commentary on Fanon, David Caute has written of the relationship between Fanon and Sartre as one in which the former substantiates much of the thought of the latter.

> Fanon's methodology is mainly implicit (and this became increasingly true in his later work) whereas Sartre's is explicit. At the same time it has to be said that a Negro is 'thrown into the world' in a total sense which escapes the white man, and therefore the testimony of a Fanon provides indispensable evidence for the wider and more complexly articulated system of a Sartre.[2]

Although it is correct that Sartre can be better understood in terms of Fanon, it will be instructive to see to what extent Fanon makes sense in terms of Sartre (and to some extent, Merleau-Ponty).[3] To accomplish this aim requires a brief outline of Sartre's conception of existential phenomenological investigation and dialectical reasoning.

It should be understood that our goal here is not to construct a causal relationship between Sartre's and Fanon's thought, but instead to identify a convergence of shared and sometimes co-extensive concerns. It is not our intent to continue the long tradition of treating the thoughts of black philosophers as derivatives of white ones.

Sartre made his early philosophical reputation as a critical proponent of Husserlian phenomenology. In his essays, *L'imagination, L'imaginaire, Le transcendance de l'ego,* and grand treatise, *L'être et le néant,* he developed his insights in phenomenology into a culminating critical ontology that amounted to a critique of traditional ontology or the study of Being. (One casualty of the Sartrean investigation is the transcendental subject, which signals the possibility of a theory that could serve as critique of the transcendental subject as a white subject.)[4]

Husserlian phenomenology, from which Sartre as well as Merleau-Ponty launched existential phenomenological analyses, involves a reduction of our everyday attitudes toward the world—what are sometimes termed our 'natural attitudes.' This reduction is not a flight *from* the world; it is instead a bracketing or suspension of certain kinds of judgment *about* the world for the purpose, ultimately, of returning to an originary or primordial reflection *on* the world. One of these bracketed judgments is the necessity of the world's existence. One can purportedly study the meaningful features of one's perception of the world without reflectively raising the question of reification or actualization.[5] Within this sphere, one's investigations take on a peculiarly psychological dimension, for at this point one is dealing with the dimensions of the world as one is conscious of those dimensions.[6] An investigation into consciousness emerges as an investigation of meaning, since the world, as apprehended in this stage, conforms to the structure of the intentional theory of consciousness: consciousness is always consciousness *of* something.

But "things" don't exist in isolation. Things are apprehended, known, and understood in relation to other things. They are, in other words, mediated. The dividing line among them is therefore a function of acts of differentiation; otherwise, the whole world would slide into a blurry, vague, one-knows-not-what.[7] At this stage, Husserlian phenomenological methodology involves an effort at free variation, at considering the various mediations of phenomena to determine "essential" features of those phenomena. In phenomenological language, this is called an "eidetic reduction," a reduction to the level of essential meaning of phenomena. It should be borne in mind that "essence" does not here mean the traditional, Aristotelian notion of an identity-relation between a thing and the property without which a thing cannot be what it "is"—that is, a substance.[8] The Husserlian sense is more praxis-epistemic in terms of its fundamental relation to the activity of phenomenological reduction; essential phenomena are *understood* as what they are in movements of active reflection toward epistemic clarity.[9]

Now, a problem emerges. As reductions occur, more and more aspects of the phenomena with which the inquirer began come into question. As less and less are presupposed, or realized as having been presupposed, the inquirer or phenomenologist begins to deal more with the objects of the suspended world in their *transcendental* dimensions—dimensions of pure meaning presupposed by the very act of seeking understanding.[10] This dimension is presented as an object of transcendental reflection—of getting to the world as *meant*. It calls, then, for a reflection *inward*, and as the story goes, this reflection "arrives" (since it apparently cannot be deduced or concluded by argumentation) at the very frame of meaning itself: transcendental consciousness of transcendental experience.[11] Husserl calls this the 'transcendental ego' and centers its investigation as the concern of phenomenological philosophy. Even in the case of his final work, *Crisis*, transcendental commitments are emphasized ultimately as having philosophical emphasis, albeit from phenomenological apprehension of the life-world as opposed to the historicist's temporalization of meaning (see his Part III).[12]

Sartre raises a number of criticisms of this conclusion, though not the point of departure. For Sartre, the calling into question the problem of consciousness was a legitimate "starting" point. All investigating involves a form of self-reflective posing of the questions, What do I see? What am I doing? Where am I?—all of which are, for Sartre, co-extensive. But Sartre adds another dimension to this question when he also asks, What is involved in my not admitting what I *see*, what I *do*, or where I supposedly *stand*? For Sartre, this is a radical—in the literal sense of *radicalis*, meaning the roots or going toward the roots—posing of the question of the questioner: the very investigation is possible only by virtue of a being that can not only question its own being, but may also deny its involvement in the questioning. It involves a being for whom *bad faith*, the effort to hide from oneself, to hide from one's freedom and responsibility, is constantly a threat, a way of being that is ultimately not *being*. It involves an existential dimension of the relationship between what is ultimately human reality and phenomena. Human being for Sartre is thus neither ontology nor ontological. Human being "is" the critique of traditional ontology. Human being positively raises the negative.[13]

Traditional ontology is, however, metaphysically theodicean; it seeks the primacy of Being, of Presence, and regards all "leaks" in Being as problems to be sealed by virtue of having been shown to be nonexistent in the first place. For Sartre, such a classical identification of nonexistence is flawed at its core, for it is an attempt to make reflective the unreflective on the level of non-reflection; it is, in effect, an attempt to transform existence into that which it is not. As Merleau-Ponty later formulates, it is an effort to make visible the invisible.[14]

The dynamics of visibility and invisibility play important roles not only in Fanon's thought, but also in the whole corpus of phenomenological efforts to describe social reality. The work of Alfred Schutz, for example, can be regarded as an effort to account for the dimensions of social reality in which we are ordinarily so steeped with familiarity that they paradoxically fail to remain familiar without estrangement.[15] The effort to reintroduce the visibility of "visible" reality often results in various typifications or interpretations of reality that eventually become confused with the phenomena they typify.[16] This is certainly the position of Sartre, Merleau-Ponty, Schutz, and, as I hope is clear thus far, Fanon.

The problem of skewed visibility, particularly when it comes to the immediacy of existential experience, is closely related to the Sartrean problem of bad faith and the phenomenological problem of critical evidencing. We have provided a preliminary formulation of Sartrean bad faith. In "Philosophy as Rigorous Science," Husserl concludes with a remark that situates the importance of the concept for phenomenological investigation a full three decades before its formal expression in Sartre's opus. "What is needed," Husserl insists, "is not the insistence that one see with his own eyes; rather it is that he not explain away under the pressure of prejudice what has been seen."[17] The "pressure of prejudice" refers to the disciplinary, institutional, and personal impediments to critical reflection which Husserl regards as radical. It is a form of investigating without being in bad faith. As Elizabeth Behnke puts it, "The phenomenological attitude, in short, suspends the dogmatic claims of any particular attitude and makes other possibilities available."[18]

It is well-known among Sartre scholars that the Sartrean analysis of bad faith makes ordinary good faith—the posture of sincerity—a form of bad faith itself. What is often overlooked, however, is that Sartre does not conclude that all forms of good faith must be rejected as forms of bad faith. In defense of the view that good faith is a form of bad faith, reference is usually made to the following famous remark from *Being and Nothingness*:

> If it is indifferent whether one is in good or in bad faith, because bad faith reapprehends good faith and slides to the very origin of the project of good faith, that does not mean that we can not radically escape bad faith. But this supposes a self-recovery of being which was previously corrupted. This self-recovery we shall call authenticity, the description of which has no place here. (p. 116, note 9)

Authenticity, then, is usually posed as an overcoming of bad faith, despite Sartre's remark that "self-recovery . . . has no place here."

It should be noted, however, that the notion of good faith is by itself ambiguous. It can allude to an unreflective or a reflective consciousness. I can believe in good faith precisely because I can be unaware of my belief's not being a form of knowledge. But I cannot reflect upon my belief, as belief, in good faith without falling into the trap of trying to make it into a form of belief that it is not (perfect belief, which is knowledge), or taking advantage of what it is (belief, which is supposedly an imperfect form of knowledge). The situation demands a critical, reflective relation to one's epistemic efforts. Sartre writes, "Bad faith does not hold the norms and criteria of truth as they are accepted *by the critical thought of good faith*" (p. 113, emphasis added).

18

There is therefore room for a critical form of good faith and, as a consequence, room for the possibility of a critical philosophy premised upon recognition of the constant threat of bad faith.

It should be evident at this point that a critical philosophy faces the dynamics of self-concealed visibility that we addressed earlier in our formulation of crisis. The revelation of concealed choices is a strike against bad faith and, as such, the problem of bad faith must be considered as a major aspect of crisis analysis.

We will here consider two matrices of bad faith—individual and institutional bad faith.[19] Individual bad faith is lived by individuals in various situations of their lives. But an individual is a complex occasion in existential phenomenology. An individual is freedom in the flesh. Whether referred to as embodied consciousness, embodied meaning, or lived body, for Sartre and Merleau-Ponty (as well as for Fanon) this amounts to the same form of being: the human being. Individual bad faith can be understood in terms of the multiple perspectives constituted by freedom in the flesh.

The human being is at least three perspectives of embodiment: the perspective from a standpoint in the world; the perspective seen from other standpoints in the world; and the human being is a perspective that is aware of itself being seen from other standpoints in the world. Sartre and Merleau-Ponty sometimes refer to these dimensions as the dimensions of the seer and the seen. We have already formulated bad faith as an effort to hide from one's freedom and responsibility. In *Being and Nothingness*, Sartre provocatively articulated the bodily dynamics of this effort as sadism and masochism.

Sadism is the effort to evade the sight of others. We can decode this goal as an effort to evade judgment. In sadism, one abstracts one's identity into complete subjectivity by ossifying all other human beings into dehumanized corporeality. In effect, the sadist conceals Others' perspectives from himself, reducing them to the level of pure materiality, flattening out their significance into a landscape of nonhuman significance. Yet his concentration on Others' embodiment abstracts from his own, until in focusing on Others, he fancies himself a pure, disembodied, anonymous subject—pure mastery, absolute negation of specificity. He fancies himself God. But since the human being is neither thing nor God, his fancy manifests an oblique reference to an eliminated humanity. The sadist is fundamentally misanthropic.

The masochist finds himself in a similar lot, although from a different point of departure. Masochism is the effort to evade oneself through attempting to become, in one's entirety, a being-for-the-sight-of-Others. The masochist literally evades himself through self-emersion. The masochist attempts to fix an eternal gaze upon himself. The masochist humiliates his own existence and deifies the Other's to the point of abstracting away the very notion of otherness. The consequence is the self-delusion of a situational thing and God—a denied humanity. The oblique reference of misanthropy reemerges.

That the sadist attempts to be an unseeable perspective and the masochist attempts to be seen without a perspective betrays an attack on sociality. For it is through the social dimensions of being, considered by standpoints beyond oneself, yet accounting for one's engagement in that consideration, of which the efforts at evasion can make sense. What could one evade in a world in which one is God? And there is certainly no point of raising the issue of evasion when one is a thing. Human beings as embodied consciousness, consciousness in the flesh, are individualized social perspectives in the world. Embodiment is simultaneously the elimination of absolute anonymity into specific matrices that constitute limited options that are necessary conditions for a meaningful life. Calvin O. Schrag makes a similar point when he writes:

> Clearly there is a socio-historical horizon to lived experience, but there also is a physico-natural horizon. Man can neither be lifted out of history nor out of nature. The task is to elucidate these horizons in such a manner that their precategorial significations come to the fore. . . . The lived-body is neither historical nor natural in the categorial sense. It is the base of operations and the center of concernful projects which envelop at the same time a sense of *lived through* history and a *concrete experience* of nature in every perceptual act, accomplishment of speech, and projection of a task. (pp. 57–58)

The situation of the human being, then, is an ambiguous relation to the active and the passive. Whatever is encountered as absolute is always subject to an interpretation whose motivating force is always the interpreter.[20] Admission of the social dimensions of embodiment is, at its core, a recognition of human being. We encounter here, then, a revision of our early formulation of the question of bad faith. Instead of asking what is involved in *my* not admitting what *I* see, we now advance to: What is involved in *our* not admitting what *we* see, or do—or admitting where *we* are?

We have come upon the question of institutional forms of bad faith. Although it is orthodox opinion in Sartre scholarship that the so-called "early" Sartre reduces sociality simply to psychological phenomena, it should be clear that sadism and masochism, *as forms of bad faith*, make no sense outside of social reality. This is not a psychological appeal. It is, in effect, a transcendental one. It is this insight that led Fanon to conclude that Sartre's descriptions of human reality in *Being and Nothingness* may be correct as long as one bears in mind that they apply fundamentally to an *alienated* consciousness, and as such they throw Sartre into the discourse of alienated sociality from Rousseau through Hegel and Marx up to Fanon himself (*Black Skin, White Masks*, p. 138, note 24).

Sociality should be immediately distinguished from collectivity. A collective does not always act socially. In the *Critique of Dialectical Reason*, Sartre uses the example of storming the Bastille to illustrate certain historical dimensions of group action.[21] We add, however, that within the moment of storming the Bastille there is a world of difference between a collective that tramples over each other along the way and one in which members stop to aid fallen comrades. In the former, the human Other has disappeared in the heat of the moment, whereas in the latter, the Other is recognized as valuable-for-himself and others.

Think also, for example, of a jazz ensemble. While warming up their instruments individually, there is merely a collection of musicians. But when the ensemble begins to play a composition, another reality

21

emerges. In order to perform music, each musician must be simultaneously aware of his own part and his fellow musicians' performances. In jazz, the group performs the melody and then each musician takes a turn at composing an extemporaneous variation on the basic theme. This form of improvisation is sometimes called "taking choruses." For our purposes, what is significant about taking choruses in jazz performances is the role of both the soloist and the accompanist. The rest of the band continues to play, but play for the purpose of "driving," that is, encouraging, the best performance out of the soloist. Simultaneously, the soloist responds to every musical suggestion made by the rest of the band. In short, a jazz performance is achieved through simultaneous, reciprocal recognition of each performer's relation to the musical performance. The music in this case is a form of sociality.

Institutional bad faith discourages human recognition. It is an effort to construct collectives and norms, "inert" practices, that militate against sociality, against human being. Although its goal is the elimination of the human in human being, its route of legitimation may be humanity-in-itself.[22] Institutional bad faith sometimes takes the form, then, of an attack on humanity in the name of humanity. Segregation in the name of order, which in turn is in the name of the peace, which in turn is in the name of the public good, which in turn is in the name of protecting the innocent, and so on. The appeal is familiar. There is a discouragement of choice through the presentation of ossified values. Slavery, segregation, apartheid, pogroms, and genocide in the name of order can take on cosmological and cosmogonic manifestations—to protect the way things are, which "is" the way things ought to be. In early, existential discourse, we confront *the spirit of seriousness*, the presentation of values as material, determined features of the world. Ideology, seriality, practico-inertia, variations on this infection of the social sphere are numerous, but in all, they point to the ready-made (presented as "given") tools of evasion.

Recall the sadist and the masochist. Both represent a disintegration of reciprocal human recognition. Correlated with this disintegration are various attitudes to social phenomena. For instance, the sadist may deny the social significance of evidence. "There is only *one* truth," he might say. His own. In a world in which he functions as the source of truth, he feels secure in believing what he wants to believe. What echoes from the irritating mouths of "Others" is the peculiar form of evidence that Sartre identifies in *Being and Nothingness* as "unpersuasive evidence." If pressed, what emerges is a fault in the *source* of the evidence. "Nothing good springeth from that well." Yet, our sadist needn't be brash about his position. He could also declare that "There *are* no truths, everything is just opinion." In a world in which there is no truth and all is opinion, one can easily evade the judgment of Others, since Others' opinions no longer really count for anything. At the other extreme, one may masochistically relinquish one's role in the constitution of values. Values stand "out there," but never "here." For the sadist, institutions (myths, laws, mores, folkways) stand as absolute conditions of what Others must be or do. For the masochist, they stand as absolute conditions of what he is or what he must do. For both, institutional bad faith furnishes "causal" or "material" explanations of the social, of the human. The world that emerges is, then, the world of the living dead, the comfortable, "happy" slave—the being who is a determined consequence of "nature."

In the world of the happy slave, no human being is responsible for human being. Human being is bound, contained, kept at bay, and held secure as a stabilized entity that supports self-delusion. Institutions take their place in a superstructural ontology that marks the irrelevance of human being. With nowhere to go, human being loses the significance of even losing a past, and hence the present may stand supreme, or versions of the past that substantiate the present may become supreme, which only reinforces the dominion of the present.[23] The result is historical decay; history loses its significance to the governing fiction of security.

Bad faith becomes a feature of all dimensions of crisis. On the level of knowledge and science, it conceals itself from belief through a value of disbelief. On the level of philosophy, it conceals itself from the existential dimension of philosophy as a struggle against nihilism. On the level of culture, it conceals itself from human participation in, and responsibility for, the course of history.

The Marxist overtones are obvious here. We find respective critical treatment of these three expressions of modern crisis in Marx's "On the Jewish Question," *The German Ideology*, and *The Manifesto of the Communist Party*. Sartre's recognition of this convergence took the form of the question, Can existentialism be reconciled with Marxism? For us, the argument has brought us to the same point. But as is now well known, Sartre's response was ultimately that even in the denigration of philosophy of existence to existential*ism*, which he regards as an ideology, there is the critical question of existence and materiality fused in the critical stance of such a declaration. The existential problem of bad faith emerges, but now it emerges in the dialectical service of a self-critical Marxism concerned with its birthright, not only to the struggle of the working class, but also to the struggle of reason itself, a struggle imbibed in the Marxist notions of *scientific* socialism and demystification.[24]

Where does Fanon stand in relation to all this?

Fanon claims, as we have seen, that the "fact of blackness" outlaws any ontological explanation. What are these facts? If the weight of history is one of them, then we ask, What force does this weight take? Fanon left the facts to speak for themselves, but I suggest that these *facts* are the very conditions of identity and historical consciousness with which Fanon was engaged in constant struggle on all fronts. I've argued elsewhere that the scenario that emerges from the fact of blackness is a projective non-seeing.[25] The "nature," if you will, of antiblack racism is to see the world according to the expectations of a racist ontology. Thus, when an antiblack racist looks at a man whom he has thought to be white but who turns out to "be" black, his consciousness of the other man's blackness becomes racially holistic; he begins to "see" the man's darkness, even if the man were an albino. If perception is a function of an historical condition—say, the array of racial ideologies that accompanies a certain epoch—then the weight of history on the life world runs the danger of slipping into historicism. This problem converges with the Husserlian crisis because humanity becomes an effect of history instead of its maker; humanity is akin to the addict who simultaneously is a consequence of past decisions but continuously reenacts them as effects. If Fanon demands new concepts while also demanding human beings to be actional, then he faces a self-critical questioning of the method involved in not only seeing human being, but also making human being. Let us explore this challenge.

Sartre and Fanon were men who were acutely aware of the simultaneous fluidity and rigidity of institutional power. Both wrestled with the oppressive, paradoxical significance of being powerfully "powerless." In Sartre's writings there are long meditations on his coming to grips with his bourgeois status in a world in which, at least from the standpoint of authenticity, losers win (see, e.g., his preface to *Wretched of the Earth*, pp. 7–31).[26] Only the oppressed, it seems, can have salvation. Sartre understood that although each individual bourgeois cannot change the relation of the bourgeoisie to the proletariat, each individual bourgeois is nevertheless responsible for such a relationship (*Being and Nothingness*, p. 554). He can either stand out of the proletariat's way, work on behalf of the proletariat revolution or try to destroy it, but in any case his project has the appearance of moral bankruptcy by virtue of the realization that the revolution is not *for him*. Similarly, Fanon knew that there are whites who may fight on behalf of racial justice, and they may even develop interesting arguments premised upon either universal racism ("Everyone is racist") or moral self-interest ("I am only doing this for the welfare of my moral integrity and my family's"), but in the end, there is the gnawing feeling that racial justice is not *for whites*. This is the heart of the problem with so-called "reverse discrimination" arguments. They are based upon the assumption that racial justice is met when one fights for the interests of whites (as if the interests of whites weren't already a feature of the structure of the antiblack world). This is no doubt the seduction and foundation of the logic deployed by most white supremacists and the reason why their arguments, however loaded, have *some* appeal to their audience. White supremacists and the like argue that whites who seek the liberation of nonwhites are ultimately fighting for a cause that is "abnormal" because it is not their own. Fanon puts it this way: "The racist in a culture with racism is therefore normal. . . . One cannot with impunity require of a man that he be against 'the prejudices of his group'" (*Toward the African Revolution*, p. 40). In 1961, he stated the situation of racial justice in more succinct, biblical terms: "'The last shall be first and the first last'" (*The Wretched of the Earth*, p. 37).

The crisis of European man emerges here as a problem that goes deeper than most of us—white, brown, or black—may be willing to admit. To be black may mean to suffer, literally and figuratively, on an everyday basis, but to be white may ultimately mean—at least when moral reflection is permitted to enter—to be condemned: ". . . it would be better for us to be a native at the uttermost depths of his misery than to be a former settler. . . . It is enough today for two French people to meet together for there to be a dead man between them" (Preface to *Wretched of the Earth*, pp. 29–30).

Although it may appear that this exaggerated conclusion has its genesis in Plato's *Republic*, where the just man in misery is supposed to be better off than the unjust man in splendor, it is more likely based on a line of reasoning from the *Notebooks for an Ethics*, Appendix B, which in turn has its roots in the crucifixion of Jesus of Nazareth. There Sartre observes that the "kind" master (in our analogy of Christian lore, the Roman soldiers who gave vinegar to Jesus, which, however sour, was still something to drink) is regarded by the slaves as more responsible for their condition because of the fact that he has treated his slaves humanely. He admits, by virtue of action, that they should not be slaves. We see the obverse in Hitler's logic in *Mein Kampf* and National Socialism. The *a posteriori* proof of the inferiority of inferior people is that one is able to degrade them. Thus, the *a posteriori* proof that Jews deserved the Final Solution is that six million of them were exterminated in concentration camps.[27] For blacks, the reasoning is the same. The proof that blacks are a slave race is the fact that they were enslaved.

The white problem, which has been serving as the leitmotif of our investigation into the crisis of European man, then, is that there doesn't seem to be any salvation for whites in a racist world once racism is admitted to be oppressive (which is the reason why some whites may choose vehemently to deny that such a world is oppressive). As Sartre observed:

> What a confession! Formerly our continent was buoyed up by other means: the Parthenon, Chartres, the Rights of Man, or the swastika. Now we know what these are worth; and the only chance of our being saved from shipwreck is the very Christian sentiment of guilt. You can see it's the end. (Preface to *The Wretched of the Earth*, p. 27)

When the Rights of Man take up company with the swastika or, for that matter, the burning cross, fulfillment of one's moral duty takes on a meaning that carries a degree of faith and commitment that dwarfs the staunchest Kantian and parallels Kierkegaard's "Abraham's Faith."[28] In Fanon's words, "... the moral law is not certain of itself" (*Black Skin, White Masks*, p. 227). Even if faith is a necessary condition for acting from one's moral duty, is it also a sufficient condition of European salvation?[29]

We return to our concern over the weight of history on identity formation. How would our existential explorations bear out on Fanon's relation to Racist Reason?

Consider Sartre's analysis of the weight of history on Jewish identity in *Anti-Semite and Jew*. A great deal of Sartre's discussion in *Anti-Semite and Jew* is built upon the *anti-Semite's* problem of antisemitism. Its major premise is that the Jew is fundamentally constituted as an object of the anti-Semite's sadistic look. Although it is true that the anti-Semite is in positions of power in antisemitic societies, Sartre's conclusion that it is the anti-Semite who makes the Jew is blatantly false. Those who adhere to Abraham's covenant have lived long before anyone decided to hate them. What the anti-Semite makes or, in phenomenological language, *constitutes* is the pejorative conception of being Jewish.

The situation of people of color is different. Although Jews may have existed before anti-Jews, it is not clear whether "blacks," "Indians," or "Orientals" existed as those identities before racist conceptions of these peoples were designated by such terms. The reasoning requires a separate work for a developed discussion but, in brief, it is possible that no African, nor Native Australian, nor Native American, nor Asian had any reason to think of himself as black, red, or yellow until Europeans found it necessary to define him as such.[30] This power of *defining* required specific conditions that were external to those people themselves. It is possible that, given the conditions emerging in Europe near the advent of slavery and exploitation on the basis of race, black and other variations of "colored" people may have emerged even if there were no people morphologically similar to the people of Africa, Australia, Asia, or North and South America, whom we have come to regard as "colored." It is this aspect of the black condition that compelled Fanon to declare, as we have seen, that there is nothing ontological about antiblack racism.

Does this mean, then, that these people don't have a history?

The answer is obviously negative—if, by having a history, we mean it in the colloquial sense.[31] Let us demarcate this sense of history with a lowercase *h*. Suppose we adopt a Hegelian sense of History— distinguished with the uppercase *H*—where the "highest" embodiment of *Geist* is situated. According to Hegel, the place and the people of History in his epoch were European Christians.[32] Today, it may be "Americans." *Geist* is where the globally dominant culture is located.

But for Hegel, this does not mean that might makes right (see *Philosophy of Right*, p. 216, paragraph 342); there is, however, another problem. He claims that "*Geist* is only what it does, and its act is to make itself the object of its own consciousness. In history its act is to gain consciousness of itself as *Geist*, to apprehend itself in its interpretation of itself to itself" (paragraph 343). Does this preclude black self-consciousness outside of the framework of a white conception of blackness? I don't see how an affirmative response can be made without being fallacious. Blacks would either become Historical through

28

their own recognition of their own History, in which case there would be at least two Histories, or they would be Historical through recognizing themselves in a way that is equivalent to the History that has already emerged. The former affirms blackness; the latter marks its elimination. But if the former were asserted, I don't see how the following query can be avoided: *Whose* History? An Hegelian would have to show that although blacks may make themselves objects of their own consciousness, and hence become self-conscious, this does not constitute, in their case, their embodying *Geist*. Such a resort is identical with the racist's credo that, ultimately, the problem with other races is the races themselves. Ordinary criteria of evidence for their equality to those who are the self-designated standpoint of all humanity are thereby rejected criteria for self-consciousness; such criteria are valid—except when applied to blacks. In such a context, is it any wonder that historians of Africans and Afrocentric historians send their messages to deaf ears? How can one have History when one is invisible *to* History?

In *The Journeying Self*, Maurice Natanson offers a phenomenological theory of being historical that falls outside the framework of the two conceptions considered thus far. "It must be understood at once," he writes, "that microcosmic history is not written at all; it has no historian. We are speaking of the life of the individual in the mundane world, and the 'we' speaking is the participant himself, each of us who lives reflectively in the midst of the social world and seeks to transcend the limits of Bad Faith" (p. 94).

Every black person *faces* history—*his* or *her* story—every day as a situation, as a choice, of how to stand in relation to oppression, of whether to live as a being subsumed by oppression or to live as active resistance towards liberation, or to live as mere indifference. This conception of history is rooted in daily life. As a consequence it has no "heroes." There is no question of elevating one's value beyond oneself into a spirit of seriousness. There is, instead, the recognition of how one's *actions* unfold into one's identity in relation to the socio-temporal location of one's experience.

We have said that racial discrimination leads to a form of existential indiscrimination; from the standpoint of antiblack racism there is
no difference between any of the following dyads—blacks versus *a*
black, *the* black versus *a* black, *blacks* versus *this* black. Fanon has already
identified this phenomenon in existential phenomenological language
as "overdeterimination." In the eyes of antiblack racists, blacks suffer a
hemorrhage in their facticity that permeates their existence into a
colored totality. A consequence is that there is no black autobiography
in antiblack worlds. To read Frederick Douglass's *Narrative of the Life of
Frederick Douglass*, or W.E.B. Du Bois's various "autobiographies," or
Malcolm X's "autobiography" means more than to look into the lives
of these men. It is to stare the black situation and the lifeworld of the
United States in the face. Their facticity is linked to the significance of
the United States beyond the sphere of the Revolutionary War, the
Emancipation Proclamation, the 13th and 14th Amendments, *Brown vs.
Board of Education of Topeka, Kansas*, or the Civil Rights Act of 1964.
Their facticity is linked to who they were in light of their choice to
recognize their relation to those moments in History. Frederick
Douglass's situation was that of once being a slave. But *Frederick
Douglass* emerged out of a clear understanding of *his* situation and *his*
facticity. The Frederick Douglass of History is one figure. The man who
made the decision to fight the slave-breaker, Covey, and to escape from
Maryland was another.

> Long before daylight, I was called to go and rub, curry, and feed
> the horses. I obeyed, and was glad to obey. But whilst thus
> engaged, whilst in the act of throwing down some blades from the
> loft, Mr. Covey entered the stable with a long rope; and just as I
> was half out of the loft, he caught hold of my legs, and was about
> tying me. As soon as I found what he was up to, I gave a sudden
> spring, and as I did so, he holding to my legs, I was brought
> sprawling on the stable floor. Mr. Covey seemed now to think he
> had me, and could do what he pleased; but at this moment—from
> whence came the spirit I don't know—I resolved to fight; and,
> suiting my action to the resolution, I seized Covey hard by the
> throat; and as I did so, I rose. He held on to me, and I to him. My

resistance was so entirely unexpected, that Covey seemed taken all aback. He trembled like a leaf. This gave me assurance, and I held him uneasy, causing the blood to run where I touched him with the ends of my fingers.[33]

When Douglass was making the decision to fight back, he was no hero. He simply knew the world that mattered to him in specific ways that limited his options but not his choices. His options were factical, mediated, and "objective" (Historical), but his choices were transcendent, immediate, and "situated" (historical). Impositions upon him may belong to a series of factors beyond his understanding, but his liberation could not be achieved without his taking account of his "role" in the process. It is bad faith to deny one's role in history.

We see a similar observation come to a head in Sartre's "Black Orpheus," his introductory essay to Léopold Sédar Senghor's edited collection of black poets on negritude, *Anthologie de la nouevelle poésie nègre et malgache*. Negritude was a literary theoretical response to antiblack racism which posited a unique black soul that was a source and function of a unique black reality of intrinsically black values.[34] Sartre saw negritude as a dialectical negation into History qua the proletarian revolution.[35] He had reflected in the *Notebooks for an Ethics*, the completion of which was abandoned by the 1950s, that "In a word, for progress to be one of the meanings of History, it has to descend into History as lived, sought for, and suffered progress" (p. 42).[36] This appeal to history as lived takes a more complex form in his discussion of the relationship between interiority and exteriority in the later *Critique of Dialectical Reason*. In the first volume, he writes:

> If History is totalisation and if individual practices are the sole ground of totalising temporalisation, it is not enough to reveal the totalisation developing in everyone, and consequently in our critical investigations, through the contradictions which both express and mask it. Our critical investigation must also show us *how* the practical multiplicity (which may be called "men" or "Humanity" according to taste) realises, in its very dispersal, its interiorisation. (p. 64)

31

So, if what the authors of negritude wanted was progress on the fight against antiblack racism, then their plight had to be understood in its lived, willed, and suffered dimensions that ironically set the stage for their liberation (progress).

Fanon was outraged. The "creators" of negritude, Fanon observed, needed not to *know* their Historical situation (*Black Skin, White Masks*, p. 135). He concluded:

> In all truth, in all truth I tell you, my shoulders slipped out of the framework of the world, my feet could no longer feel the touch of the ground. Without a Negro past, without a Negro future, it was impossible for me to live my Negrohood. Not yet white, no longer wholly black, I was damned. Jean-Paul Sartre had forgotten that the Negro suffers in his body quite differently from the white man. Between the white man and me the connection was irrevocably one of transcendence. (p. 138)

Fanon's conclusion affirmed Sartre's verdict on the negritude-fortified black's relation to History—that if the black's cry were to be heard as a cry, it would not be a black one (p. 29). History (with upper-case *H*) already had, and continues to have, a "place" for black women and men. "However painful it may be for me to accept this conclusion," Fanon confesses, "I am obliged to state it: For the black man there is only one destiny. And it is white" (p. 10). There is no hope, from Fanon's point of departure, for the black man to gain another "place."[37] For his blackness, recognized as such, renders such a feat no more than a *coup* (pp. 11 and 30). What both Fanon and Sartre began to see in the late forties and ultimately saw by the mid-fifties was that revolutionary considerations were needed for a *human* place in the story of self-consciousness that stands outside of white superiority and colored inferiority. This is the thesis of *A Dying Colonialism*, where Fanon shows how a transformation of consciousness emerges through mass mobilization in revolutionary praxis.[38] One should bear in mind, however, that Fanon's thesis related to his appeal to humanism and humanization is premised upon the provision of the source of revolution being rooted in the situation and experience of the colonized—that is, the oppressed.

Theorists of revolution like C.W. Cassineli who regard "total revolutions" as fundamentally "totalitarian" fail to account for the distinction between revolution and liberation. Chairman Mao's objectives were fundamentally different from Hitler's, and even Stalin's, by virtue of how the Chinese stood in relation to the West. Thus, the designation "Stalin, Hitler, and Mao" is a serious distortion of reality. Fanon's form of revolution is one that is fundamentally liberatory or liberating praxis.

"Black Orpheus" must therefore be rejected because of an obvious flaw which Sartre slips into the general racist, dyadic matrices of whiteness in the world of reason, and blackness in the world of affect. It is not, as one might be inclined to think, that he attempts to reduce blacks to the proletariat. It is instead that he seeks to *elevate* blacks to such a level. He appears to have been aware of the "under-class" status of blacks. He seems in this case to have abandoned his general project of exposing the spirit of seriousness, for even though negritude reflected an under-class designation, it also reflected a form of Manichaeism—the material anti-value of blackness in the face of whiteness. Even if it were pointed out that Sartre regarded negritude as a relative attitude instead of an objective value—which means that he was not to regard it as what the proponents of negritude considered it to be—it must be remembered that he also regarded the white working class as an objective value as, in fact, History. The problem of seriousness stands writ large.[39]

Fanon regarded the situation of each man to be a constant struggle against the degradation of Man. "I find myself suddenly in the world and I recognize that I have one right alone: That of demanding human behavior form the other. One duty alone: That of not renouncing my freedom through my choices. . . . I, the man of color, want only this: That the tool never possess the man. That the enslavement of man by man cease forever. . . . That it be possible for me to discover and to love man, wherever he may be" (*Black Skin, White Masks*, pp. 229–231). In his letter of resignation from his position as *chef de service* at the Blida-Joinville psychiatric clinic, he summarized the existential situation of the psychiatrist in a colonial society.

For many months my conscience has been the seat of unpardon-
able debates. And their conclusion is that I cannot continue to bear
a responsibility at no matter what cost, on the false pretext that there
is nothing else to be done. (*Toward the African Revolution*, p. 53)

The way Fanon lived his situation in 1956 was not only by
resigning, but also by placing himself in the service of the revolutionary
forces of Algeria.

Fanon has shown that the white stands in front of the black as the
master *in an antiblack world*, in the Historical world. Although he has not
shown that the relation is contingent, he believes the relation is a consequence of a contingent Historical situation. We find ourselves in the
epoch of a racist world, but other kinds of worlds have existed and *could*
exist in the future. His liberation project demands that the relation of
the white to the colored be contingent. In short, the *struggle* for racial
justice requires such a possibility. Otherwise, how would "This [veiled
Algerian] woman who sees without being seen frustrates the colonizer"
make sense?[40] In his discussion of class-struggle in *The Critique of
Dialectical Reason*, Sartre makes a similar point: "But this serial, practico-
inert statute [roughly, a stratified, oppressed group identity] would not
lead to class *struggle* if the permanent possibility of dissolving the series
were not available to everyone; and we have seen how a first, abstract
determination of this possible unity emerges through class interest, as a
possible negation of destiny" (p. 679).

Fanon declares that "[Society,] unlike biochemical processes,
cannot escape human influence. Man is what brings society into
being. . . . The black man must wage his war on both levels: Since
[H]istorically they influence each other, any unilateral liberation is
incomplete, and the gravest mistake would be to believe in their auto-
matic interdependence" (*Black Skin, White Masks*, p. 11). To this we add
that what is contingent need not be accidental. History (all three kinds)
has shown that a subjugated black race was no accident. Two years later,
in his analysis of the Antillean and the African, Fanon takes the existential phenomenological standpoint of analyzing racial phenomena
from the standpoint of bad faith and, in effect, substantiates our

criticism of his earlier position through admitting the importance of an analysis that differentiates contingency from "deeper" levels of philosophically significant phenomena:

> I shall be found to use terms like "metaphysical guilt," or "obsession with purity." I shall ask the reader not to be surprised: these will be accurate to the extent to which it is understood that since what is important cannot be attained, or more precisely, since what is important is not really sought after, one falls back on what is contingent. This is one of the laws of recrimination and of bad faith. The urgent thing is to rediscover what is important beneath what is contingent. (*Toward the African Revolution*, p. 18)

This realization is often overlooked in contemporary, ultimately poststructuralist approaches to the study of Fanon and the study of race.[41]

So we have arrived at some concluding remarks.

First, Fanon embodies the crisis of European man as a crisis of value. Unlike the Nietzschean transvaluation of value, Fanon's position is acutely aware of the affordability of power. Nietzsche, as the ironic embodiment of European man, is the man who cannot justify himself. Fanon, as the embodiment of the *crisis* of European man, is the man who is wrongfully expected to state his own justification. Second, Fanon's thought emerges as a form of critical philosophy, a philosophy critical of the West within the West. Fanon's critical philosophy is a reflection upon Western society from within Western society as his life-world ironically situates his thought within the specific Western matrix of existential phenomenological critique. As a radical humanist, however, he stands in a critical relation to ontology. He rejects all ontology that puts existence to the wayside. His sentiment is fundamentally existential. But Fanon's critical stand demands a "high-level," rigorous, critical, self-reflective praxis. This is the case in his analysis of language in *Black Skin, White Masks,* and the pitfalls of national character and the use of violence in *The Wretched of the Earth*.[42] Philosophically, then, he demands a conception of the human sciences that rejects an ontologized nature. I offer the hermeneutical significance of bad faith, premised upon human being as fundamentally open, as a clue.

THREE

Racism, Colonialism, and Anonymity: Social Theory and Embodied Agency

Flesh and blood values may not be as universal or objective as logical truths and schematized judgments, but they are not thereby
deprived of some relative objectivity and universality of their
own. . . . They are not grounded in types of realms of value, but are
rooted in modes or kinds of *valuing*.
            —Alain Locke, *The Philosophy of Alain Locke*

Phenomenology does not simply displace subjectivity, à la the "death
of man" theme of structuralism; it launches a disciplined inquiry into
the genealogy of subjectivity and objectivity alike, as they emerge
from a precategorial life-world. And already in phenomenology,
particularly in its third-generation expression in the thought of
Merleau-Ponty and Alfred Schutz, we discern a move beyond both
the formalism of a transcendental ego and the idiosyncratic historic-
ity of a personal subject to the socio-historical formative context
which encompass human thought and action.
            —Calvin O. Schrag, *Radical Reflection*

What enables us to centre our existence is also what prevents us from
centering it completely, and the anonymity of our body is insepara-
bly both freedom and servitude. Thus, to sum up, the ambiguity of
being-in-the-world is translated by that of the body, and this is understood through that of time.
            —Merleau-Ponty, *Phenomenology of Perception*

WE HAVE thus far identified the crisis of European man as a form of bad faith.[1] In response to such bad faith, we have identified Fanon as a philosopher who demands a forward leap on the question and questioning of humanity. At this point, we consider the question: What constitutes moving forward for Fanon? To answer this question, we shall examine two phenomena toward the overcoming of which Fanon devoted considerable energy: racism and colonialism.

There are many ways to speak of racism. We have already discussed one—racism as a form of bad faith. Now, let us look at an implication of this conception. We have argued that racism is a form of lying about oneself and others that is nurtured and encouraged by the very institutions of racist society. Our thesis leads to perhaps the most insidious feature of racism: its mundanity. Fanon writes that "Psychologists spoke of a prejudice having become unconscious. The truth is that the rigor of the system made the daily affirmation of a superiority superfluous" (*Toward the African Revolution*, p. 37). It is a short step to the conclusion that "The racist in a culture with racism is therefore normal" (p. 40).

With racism's permeation of daily life, grandiose assaults on racism—highly public spectacles against exceptional behavior—miss the mark. Racism, as a function of extraordinary individuals conceals the structural dimension of a society that conceals itself from itself through making its noxious values so familiar and frequent that they cease to function as objects of observation and reflection; they, in short, become unreflective and so steeped in familiarity that they become invisible.

The phenomenological articulation of the relation between familiarity and invisibility is most explicit in the work of Alfred Schutz and Maurice Natanson.[2] Both Schutz and Natanson locate these phenomena in the everyday world, the ordinary world, the lifeworld. In the everyday world in which we live our ordinary, mundane lives, there is an element of frequency that defers reflection—even at times to the ironic posture of unreflective reflection—to the wayside. For example, commuters often discover, after a period of driving to work each morning and driving home each evening, that their consciousness of going through the mechanics of driving—accelerating with traffic, stopping at red lights, driving cautiously around curves, avoiding bikers and pedestrians—falls into a fog of indistinction and nonreflection. It is as if the commuter simply steps into the car and suddenly finds himself at the job or at home. Or we can consider the case of the block on which one lives. One sometimes finds oneself "discovering" buildings that occupy spaces that seemed nonexistent before their discovery—the decrepit home next to the beautiful one on the corner, the funeral home next to the string of houses.

The everyday dimension of racism in a racist society breeds a comfortable facticity of bad faith. Racist institutions are designed so as to facilitate racism with the grace of walking through air on a calm summer's day. Reality is racialized and rationalized with racist categories so as to permeate the very core of explanation; like fish in water, being "wet" loses all points of reference.

I once attended a symposium at a conference of American philosophers at which a white speaker advocated the thesis that the affirmation of a black identity by black people has to be held at fault for the derailment of black liberation struggles of the 1960s. Had black people simply given up their affirmation of a black identity, he argued, they would have been more accessible to a unified, working-class struggle against racism and poverty. We have already discussed some of the problems of this view in our treatment of Sartre's efforts in "Black Orpheus." But unlike the speaker at this conference, Sartre never advocated the view that black people's affirmation of their black identity is an impediment to their liberatory goals. On the contrary, Sartre's view, as we've seen, is that it is a necessary condition in an important dialectical struggle. Moreover, neither Sartre nor Fanon espoused the view that black identity poses a *black* problem. The problem rests within the antiblack racist's response to black presence. The speaker's argument ultimately responds to problems of race by placing the burden of racial tension upon black people; in effect, he demanded their phenomenological disappearance. After the conference, discussion emerged on the offensiveness of the paper. But eyebrows were raised when I referred to the speaker's position as racist. The speaker was a self-claimed Marxist activist who taught at a black university. How could he be racist? My response was an appeal to the zeal with which he defended a racist form of *explanation*. In the face of the historical fact of FBI and CIA demolition of working-class and race-based movements in the 1950s, '60s, and '70s, the speaker's response was to look at black people as the cause of such sabotage and tribulation. Fanon's work is rich with critical assessments of examples of this dimension of racism, examples that we will see unfold in the course of our discussion. For now, what is of concern is that in a racist world there is a constant search for the positioning of racial pathologies versus the critical evaluation of racist structures that encourage pathological interpretations. In Fanon's words:

> Here one perceives the mechanism of explanation that, in psychiatry, could give us this: There are latent forms of psychosis that become overt as the result of a traumatic experience. Or, in somatic medicine, this: The appearance of varicose veins in a patient does not arise out of his being compelled to spend ten hours a day on his feet, but rather out of the constitutional weakness of his vein walls; his working conditions are only a complicating factor. And the insurance compensation expert to whom the case is submitted will find the responsibility of the employer extremely limited. (p. 85)

Racist explanations are so much a part of the intellectual fiber of a racist society that, like the legitimacy of common sense, they are taken for granted as valid.

"Nigger women are so promiscuous," observed a traveler on a Southern plantation during slavery. "Look at all the pregnant pickaninnies."[3]

One can point out that young women who are deemed to be

property hardly have any options over the matter of their sexual violation.[3]

"The blacks are a violent lot. Look at all the black-on-black violence they perpetrate on each other."

One can point out that people tend to harm those whom they know and, given the fact that many black people in low social-economic urban environments tend to know mostly blacks, it would be odd if most of the people they harm turn out to be white. "White-on-white" crime is an invisible feature of the mundane racist world. Inadequacy, failure, perversion, pathology, weakness, irrationality, and a host of deficiencies are projected into the so-called inferior race to make their inferiority cause and effect:

> When you examine at close quarters the colonial context, it is evident that what parcels out the world is to begin with the fact of belonging to or not belonging to a given race, a given species. In the colonies the economic substructure is also a superstructure. The cause is the consequence; you are rich because you are white, you are white because you are rich. (*The Wretched of the Earth*, p. 40)

> It is utopian to expect the Negro or the Arab to exert the effort of embedding abstract values into his outlook on the world when he has barely enough food to keep alive. To ask a Negro of the Upper Niger to wear shoes, to say of him that he will never be a Schubert, is no less ridiculous than to be surprised that a worker in the Berliet truck factory does not spend his evenings studying lyricism in Hindu literature or to say that he will never be an Einstein. (*Black Skin, White Masks*, pp. 95–96)

Implicit in Fanon's focus on the everyday is the following view of oppression. Oppression is the imposition of extraordinary conditions of the ordinary upon individuals in the course of their effort to live "ordinary" lives. Recall our ascription of obscenity to the well-adjusted black or slave in an antiblack or slave-structured society. "Because it is a systematic negation of the other person and a furious determination to deny the other person all attributes of humanity, colonialism forces the people it dominates to ask themselves the question constantly:'In reality, who am I?' (*The Wretched of the Earth*, p. 250) In place of 'colonialism,' 'racism' works just as well here. The black or the woman who asks constantly, "Am I good enough for this job?"; "Do I belong here?"; "What is wrong with me and my kind?" The very construction of employment, healthcare, safe housing, safe travel, raising children, and a great number of the mundane features of "reasonable" day-to-day living demands extraordinary choices and efforts to be lived mundanely. There is the mundane for the white and the mundane for the black. A black who achieves white mundanity would be one who has accomplished no slight task, for admission to white mundanity is deemed available only to the "best" blacks. "'Look at the nigger! . . . Mama, a Negro!' . . . 'Hell, he's getting mad.' . . . 'Take no notice, sir, he does not know that you are as civilized as we. . . .'" (*Black Skin, White Masks*, p. 113); "'Oh, I want you to meet my black friend. . . . Aimé Césaire, a black man and a university graduate. . . . Marian Anderson, the finest of Negro singers. . . . Dr. Cobb, who invented white blood, is a Negro. . . . Here, say hello to my friend from Martinique (be careful, he's extremely sensitive) . . . .'" (p. 116)

Fanon dreams of a liberating transformation of the everyday. "All I wanted was to be a man among other men. I wanted to come lithe and young into a world that was ours and to help to build it together" (pp. 112–113). In this world:

> I can imagine myself lost, submerged in a white flood composed of men like Sartre or Aragon, I should like nothing better. . . . But I do not feel that I should be abandoning my personality by marrying a European, whoever she might be; I can tell you that I am making no "fool's bargains." If my children are suspected, if the crescents of their fingernails are inspected, it will be simply because society will not have changed, because, as you so well put it, society will have kept its problem from the standpoint of *either-or.* (*Black Skin, White Masks*, pp. 202–203)

A liberating transformation of the everyday involves an absence of representative blackness. For in such a world, black presence would be no more unusual than any other presence in the world; it would, in short, be mundane. What emerges at this point is the thesis that oppression and liberation are both functions of peculiar forms of anonymity. Anonymity means to be "nameless." In social theory, particularly the Husserlian-based social theory found in the philosophies of Schutz and Natanson, it refers to more complex phenomena to which we will shortly turn. For now, let it be said that if the black has mundane access to the mundane, then the contours of subjectivity are such that standpoint and identity epistemological conceptions need to be regarded as limited: one's standpoint and "identity" are helpful, but not total. One can place oneself in another's place.

The ability to put oneself in another's place raises questions about the absoluteness, the ontological rigidity, of one's situation. For if the-place-of-the-Other is an ever-present possibility, then so, too, is one's place vis-à-vis the Other. One is an Other's Other. Thus stated, we find the uniqueness of our circumstances subject to a peculiar sense of anonymity—it takes on a form that may not be uniquely our own, although there is a very real sense in which it is our own by virtue of the fact that we are the ones who are living it at the time of consideration.

I have thus far been articulating an existential-phenomenological interpretation of what Fanon means by moving forward on problems of oppression and liberation. No doubt some readers will raise their eyebrows because a philosopher of existence leads a lonely life among philosophers in this day and age (although in my experience this circumstance is offset by the continued enthusiasm of students for the subject). Kierkegaard faced the Present Age, Buber faced anti-Semitism culminating in the Holocaust, Sartre faced The Occupation, Fanon faced racism, colonialism, and global dehumanization. That Fanon has articulated his philosophical positions in contexts of liberating struggle might make his convergence with existential philosophy seem almost absurd to those who may regard existential thought as a form of naïve humanism (Heidegger, Lyotard), linguistic and stylistic rubbish (Carnap and Adorno), naïve bourgeois individualism (Lukács and Marcuse), or wretched nihilism.

43

A black philosopher of existence finds himself sitting in a corridor of a university during a conference. He is tired but still willing to engage in conversation about "work."

"What are you working on?" emerges a voice out of the hum of conference chatter.

"A book. It's entitled *Fanon and the Crisis of European Man*."

"Hmmm. What do you mean by crisis?" (In the academic world—particularly its philosophical incarnations—this can be termed "the set up.")

"There are many meanings," answers our philosopher, "but the traditional one is sufficient: a form of indecision in the face of decision. I argue that it's a form of bad faith."

"Bad faith? What do you mean by bad faith?"

"I mean specifically Sartrean bad faith, which is a form of lying to oneself in an effort to escape freedom, responsibility, and human being."

"A book on existential philosophy, heh?" A moment's pause. "Isn't existentialism a sort of post-war European *Angst*, an outdated philosophy in which Europe tries to come to grips with its lost place of world domination?"

Our philosopher's eyes narrow. "Do you mean like postmodernism today?" These days, those are fighting words.

"Touché."

Our philosopher shows some courtesy. "It is important to distinguish existentialism from the philosophy of existence. The former represents an ideological moment in the history of ideas that is well suited to the description you've offered. But philosophy of existence is another matter. Whatever conceptual framework it is that sets the stage for European *Angst*, it is an error to assume that such a conceptual framework precedes the experiences people suffer. Philosophy of existence comes out of experiences like our feeling responsible for situations that are clearly not our fault, or questions like the following: Why is it that we are simultaneously affected by the weight of social structures and the sense that we constitute those structures? How is liberation possible? Anguish didn't emerge in World War I and World War II. You can find it in Abraham's trip to Mount Moriah, or Sojourner Truth's decision to resist, to rebel, to fight." (There is something about liberation discourse that sometimes invites pontification.)

"Yeah," retorts the colleague, "but what does all that prove? Why haven't many black philosophers identified themselves as existentialists?"

"It is a mark of existential philosophy that although there are many thinkers who may use its line of critique, only a few of them constitute existential philosophers to begin with," responds our philosopher. "Neither Kierkegaard, Buber, nor especially Heidegger, called themselves existentialists. But they can easily be found in discussions of a small set of thinkers who include Sartre and de Beauvoir. An existential standpoint rests upon the following theses: that the lived body is the subject of agency instead of subjects like the abstract Kantian transcendental subject; that the fundamental problem of value is the problematization of self and other; and that anguish over freedom and the reality of unfreedom poses problems of liberation. One need only find black philosophers who hold these theses and one will encounter, regardless of their self-ascription, existential philosophers."[4]

We have shown thus far that, in Fanon's view, however universal the hostile structures against black presence may be, we must also remember that all of those structures are *situationally* lived by people of flesh and blood. This appeal (among the theses listed) situates Fanon's thought in existential philosophy and in terms of method, in existential phenomenology. But in situating Fanon in the realm of existential phenomenology, we face a number of problems. The first is a function of Fanon's rejection of ontology, and that problem is the question of an anthropology that succeeds existence. We confront certain realities of the social world, including its sociogenesis.

Fanon's method utilizes a great deal of phenomenological technique. Witness the descriptions of human reality under conditions of oppression that we have been identifying throughout our discussion. Why did Fanon take a *phenomenological* route in his investigations? One argument is that such a route was the only conceptual tool available to him at that time. He was an intellectual who was trained in the French tradition, and France in the 1940s and 1950s was dominated by the thought of Sartre, de Beauvoir, Merleau-Ponty, Jean Wahl, Raymond Aron, and Francis Jeanson, all of whom were influenced by Husserl. The problem with such an argument, however, is that it only suspends the question instead of answering it, since the same problem pertains to the European philosophers of that period: Why did *they* explore human reality from the standpoint of existential phenomenology or phenomenological ontology (critical ontology)?

Fanon chose his conceptual tools for the same reason his European contemporaries chose theirs: because of the type of problems that concerned them. Fanon warned that "society, unlike biochemical processes, cannot escape human influences. Man is what brings society into being" (*Black Skin, White Masks*, p. 11). Man is ontologically prior to his conceptualization; his existence, that is, precedes his essence. Once placed in motion as an object of inquiry, however, his "essence" is sometimes essentialized in such a way as to become a prior ontology. Human products become human causes. As a student of human reality, then, the social theorist faces the problem of studying that which cannot escape human influence. This problem is made worse when the attempt is made to study the "agent" who is the condition of the "object" of inquiry: the human being. The very "objects" of study, if you will, stand like universal propositions in Boolean logic—"empty" sets. For example, in the case of studying blacks, Fanon observes:

> The object of lumping all Negroes together under the designation of "Negro people" is to deprive them of any possibility of individual expression. What is thus attempted is to put them under the obligation of matching the idea one has of them. Is it not obvious that there can only be a white race? What would the "white people" correspond to? (*Toward the African Revolution*, p. 17)

Whatever "Negro people" *are*, living, breathing, flesh-and-blood black folk have to go on with their lives and day-to-day problems within culturally different contexts. Fanon's path was marked, then, by the same calling that drove philosophers of social science and culture—philosophers like Schutz in Europe and the Marxist philosopher, Paulin Hountondji, in Africa—to phenomenological treatments of culture.[5] Granting that certain conceptions of human reality, like race and racism, are unmasked as bogus claims—that they are, in contemporary parlance, social constructions—it is also important for us to understand that such a conclusion is not the end of the issue, but the beginning of a whole set of new problems. When it is asserted that race is a social construct, the question is also raised, What does that mean? Who *constructs* it? A social construction is meaningless without that to which it is opposed. We will find ourselves in a trap if we propose the purely natural or the physical as our non-social alternative. For all we would show is that there is no extensional, prior-reality of race. But then, so what? We *know* that the importance of race is a function of racial and racist *concern*—as we have seen in our examples of racist explanations. It is, in effect, a value to which, like it or not, "we" are committed as a racist society. The term 'social construct' only identifies society as a constitutor of race. But that tells us nothing if we do not understand how, in such an instance, a society can create anything. To construct society suprastructurally (above or beyond human involvement) would manifest a failure to heed Fanon's warning, which we shall here repeat, that "society, unlike biochemical processes, cannot escape human influences. Man is what brings society into being." The ascription of agency to the amorphous societal subject hides itself as metaphor in such instances. For society, in such a case, is a projection of the anonymous individual who serves as the microcosmic version of macrocosmic agency. Here we find complete agreement between individual and societal reality. We have been arguing thus far that such an agreement, as in the case of Fanon's normal racist, is a classic case of the serious spirit.

The concept of the social constructivity of race is of no value without a prior understanding of what is involved in the construction of any phenomenon. Social construction is a vague way of saying

47

"societally constituted." But as we have been spelling out, "societally constituted" is itself a problematic term, since society is a rather shy agent. It prefers to remain anonymous.

A theory of agency is central for the identification not only of the oppressor, but also of the oppressed. The theory of agency that we have been espousing, as well as attributing to Fanon through existential phenomenology, is a theory premised upon *de facto* action, upon who, literally, acts.

The classic formulation of action as a function of agency can be found in the work of Max Weber, who writes:

> In "action" is included all human behavior when and in so far as the acting individual attaches a subjective meaning to it. Action in this sense may be either overt or purely inward or subjective; it may consist of positive intervention in a situation, or of deliberately refraining from such intervention or passively acquiescing in the situation. Action is social in so far as, by virtue of the subjective meaning attached to it by the acting individual (or individuals), it takes account of the behavior of others and is thereby oriented in its course.[6]

Wittgenstein once posed the question of the distinction between a hand being raised and raising a hand. Given Weber's description of action, we can say here that the first gesture constitutes mere behavior, whereas the second constitutes action. From the standpoint of an extensional language like that of physics or natural science, there is no difference between these two cases, primarily because what is observed is considered solely from the standpoint of the third person. In order to "see" action, one has to be able to get "inside," so to speak; one has to be able to get to the subjective element that marks a central feature of behavior that is also action. But now we face a whole philosophical can of worms, from Descartes to Sartre, and that is the problem—or perhaps more accurately, the problematization—of other selves. This is not the place for detailed discussion of this problem. We have already stated our position in our discussion of bad faith, that to reject the Other as a perspective from which we are constituted as Other is an effort to evade our own experience; in short, it is a form of bad faith. In effect, we stand clear in this move from the tendency to conflate what Natanson calls "concrete we-relationships" with "pure we-relationships" (*Anonymity*, p. 14). On this matter, Schutz provides some insight:

> The Thou-orientation is the general form in which any particular fellow-man is experienced in person. The very fact that I recognize something within the reach of my direct experience as a living, conscious human being constitutes the Thou-orientation. In order to preclude misunderstandings, it must be emphasized that the Thou-orientation is not a judgment by analogy. Becoming aware of a human being confronting me does not depend upon an imputation of life and consciousness to an object in my surroundings by an act of reflective thought. The Thou-orientation is a prepredicative experience of a fellow being.[7]

Here we find complete agreement with Fanon's view that problematization of concrete encounters with others represents an alienated reality. But here, too, we see the importance of the lived body as both point-of-action or agent. When Fanon speaks of agent or actor or consciousness or human being, he means the concrete individuals we encounter in mundane experience.

"The problem here is that I don't quite see what you mean by agency," said a critic at lunch after a conference in which I presented segments of this work.

"You and all the people sitting at this table, as well as the people going about their lives around us and in the rest of the world," was my response, but consider, also, Natanson's version of the same point:

> The ontological givenness of the Other in concrete we-relations cannot be spun out of a pure, *a priori*, or transcendental "We." Nor can the "We" be *created* out of the ego, however primordial or powerful that ego may be in its transcendental character. That the concrete person who is my Other in a face-to-face relationship is indeed an individual means that individuation is bitterly ambiguous [think, for example, of Merleau-Ponty here], for "an

individual" is what every individual is and is not. The pure we-relationship accommodates "an individual" who is, typically, perceived as "someone encountered." Ontologically speaking, however, the concreteness of the individual is unsubstitutable, the encounter is unrepeatable, the person and the moment are absolute. (*Anonymity*, pp. 16–17)

The concrete "cause," if you will, of action is the agent who acts: human beings, freedoms, in the flesh.

In *The Problem of Social Reality*, Schutz defines social reality as "the sum total of objects and occurrences within the social, cultural world as experienced by the common-sense thinking of men living their daily lives among their fellow-men, connected with them in manifold relations of interaction" (p. 53). A conclusion of the Weberian, Sartrean, Schutzean, and, we shall now add, Fanonian conception of action, then, is that social reality is an achievement, not a given reality. It is a function of action, itself a function of subjective and intersubjective encounter. From this standpoint, the notion of *social* constructs suffers another blow—the charge of redundancy; appeal to social constructions is redundant for the mere fact that sociality is itself constructed.[8]

We find ourselves again facing the question of agency, that is, identifying the agent of social construction and the construction of social reality. For Fanon, there is no problem in acknowledging the human being's place here, and he is vehement in his rejection of the mechanistic spirit that rejects the actional, subjective, situated dimension of human being. We'll quote him at length:

> What are by common consent called the human sciences have their own drama. Should one postulate a type of human reality and describe its psychic modalities only through deviations from it, or should one not rather strive unremittingly for a concrete and ever-new understanding of man? When one reads that after the age of twenty-nine a man can no longer love and that he must wait until he is forty-nine before his capacity for affect revives, one feels the ground give way beneath one. The only possibility of

regaining one's balance is to face the whole problem, for all these discoveries, all these inquiries lead only in one direction: to make man admit that he is nothing, absolutely nothing—and that he must put an end to the narcissism on which he relies in order to imagine that he is different from the other "animals." This amounts to nothing more nor less than *man's surrender.* Having reflected on that, I grasp my narcissism with both hands and I turn my back on the degradation of those who would make man a mere mechanism. (*Black Skin, White Masks*, pp. 22–23)

Natural scientific discourse provides a convenient model of an exact discourse. Its objects of study amount to those for which one can work within the confines of "all there is." But the language of all-there-is, a language wiped clean of ambiguity, is a language in which there is a one-to-one relation between name and named. In effect, it is an extensional language not only of essences, but also of essentialized reality; a language, that is, of substances. The appeal is made vivid in the work of Gottlob Frege.[9] Frege pointed out that there is a distinction between a referent (what is sometimes called an extension) and its senses (what are sometimes called intensions or meanings). A particular referent can have more than one sense (meaning), but there may only be one referent (or at times no referent) for some terms that may have senses. The familiar example is the morning star and the evening star, which are two different meaningful names for the same referent, the planet Venus. Now, the limitation of building a theory upon sense instead of reference is easily shown by the fact that some terms may have senses, but no referents, like the familiar example of Pegasus, the mythological flying horse, or, given the course of our discussion thus far, *race*.[10] At least with referents, the argument goes, we are assured some basis in reality, and from there we find the familiar litany of analytical and positivist theories of human science from John Stuart Mill through Sir Karl Popper and Willard Van Orman Quine (who defended the thesis of a purely extensional language in all the sciences).[11] But even in such circles, there are heretics. For example:

In recent years, I have been trying to ground the theory of speech acts in the theory of the mind, specifically in the theory of Intentionality. . . . I think that most researchers would agree that the general project must be right, because we know in advance that speech acts are a subclass of human actions, and thus we should be able to state what speech acts have in common with human actions in general simply in virtue of being acts and how they are special, how they differ by way of being speech acts. We know, furthermore, that human actions are themselves expressions of human Intentionality: intentions, beliefs, desires, etc.[12]

Here one wonders whether John Searle has ever heard the name Edmund Husserl. He continues:

What is added when we say that the speaker not only intentionally *uttered* "It is raining" but he *meant* that it is raining? Well, normally he will have had the intention to perform a certain type of *speech act,* to make the *statement* that it is raining. He did not just intend to utter a sentence, but he intended to utter that sentence by way of making [a] statement. . . . But what I am trying to analyze here are the very bare bones of that component of the intention to make a statement which includes the essential aspect of our pretheoretical notion of saying something and *meaning* something. And the answer I am proposing is the common sense one: the very bare bones of the intention to state are the intention that one's utterance should be *meaningful* in the quite specific sense that it should be a *representation* of a state of affairs. (p. 83)

Given these ruminations on what is ultimately the phenomenological problem of the constitution of meaning, affinities with Weber, Schutz, and Fanon are not far off:

I have argued that in explaining human behavior we need both a mentalistic and a neurophysiological level of explanation. Within each of these levels there will, in all likelihood, be many sublevels. Thus, for example, in the Intentionalistic explanation of human behavior we need to account for both the levels of individual Intentionality and collective Intentionality. We need the individual level if, for example, we are trying to explain why a particular human being engages in a certain course of action. But if, for example, we are examining wars, revolutions, or collective economic behavior, we will also have to investigate collective forms of Intentionality. . . . [I]f my particular account of Intentionality is correct, it has the consequence that we do not have laws in the social sciences comparable to the sorts of laws that we have in physics and chemistry. (p. 335)

Searle goes on to point out that social phenomena "are only the phenomena they are if people think they are those phenomena." In phenomenological language, Searle seeks to show that objective meaning of social phenomena—that to which social-scientific investigation refers—can only be understood in terms of an ultimate appeal to subjective meaning. At issue is what is intended. That "what" is not a referent "in" the world, but instead a slew of simultaneous intended meanings. "What is intended" may be a multitude of significations in a single act: the consumption of food can also be one of orgasmic sexual delight; the raising of a hand can also be a call for a taxi, which can also be an effort to arrive early for an important meeting, which can also be an effort to avoid the problem of dealing with "dangerous people" on the subways; or lying down to rest can simultaneously be a way of delaying a visit to a friend to deliver bad news, etc.

But now we have arrived at another concern. If human reality carries a multitude of meanings, how is it possible to make descriptions of human beings without slipping into limited conceptions, reduced singular-meaning references—in fine, essences? Further, if we grant that it is difficult to talk about social reality without employing some use or mention of essences, there is still, however, the question of what kind of essences comprise the social world? Can essences be used without essentialization or essentializing?

At this point, the turn to phenomenology can be appreciated. In our discussion of Husserlian phenomenology, we briefly identified the type of essences in question as constituted essences, as opposed to Aristotelian essences (which are substances). The constitution of such essences introduces a number of difficulties. Among these difficulties is the problem of whether any appeal to essences is symptomatic of a failure to apprehend fully the nature of the crisis with which we are dealing. Granting that we are dealing with essences that are realized as constructed realities, the "crisis" element of our discussion focuses on the self-reflective apprehension of identity-constitution on the level of value—in other words, on the constructor in the act of constructing constructions. How do we get at this phenomenon? If we fail to get at it, why not jettison even the value of constructivity apprehension? Can we ever deconstruct our constructions radically enough?

Part of the problem of achieving radicality rests on the difficulty of identifying our presumptions in our inquiry at hand. We may in fact seek the atypical in very typical ways. This problem calls for some explication of the role of typification in social theory.

Consider the token/type distinction, one that is a popular point of departure. In trigonometry classes, it is instructive to use a visual aid to illustrate the variety of triangular or trilateral phenomena under study. The "triangles" used in classes to exemplify triangles are not, however, ideal instances of triangles. The presented figures are tokens for the types that constitute triangles. Whereas it is coherent to count, for instance, how many tokens of a right triangle are drawn on a given blackboard, it is incoherent to ask how many there are of the type, *right triangle*. The problem becomes like the treatment of the number one as a proper name. Although two "ones" constitute the number "two," it is incoherent to refer to any of these "ones" as a unique number "one."[13]

But suppose we decide to examine the tokens themselves. With such focus, we will arrive at different conclusions than we would have if we were attempting to get at the type, *triangle-in-itself.* The tokens represent a proximate instead of exact reality. Thus, tokens tell us about a world whose typification is not absolute. It can be otherwise.

In the realm of social theory, we face a similar concern. For there is no type of "human being" that is prior to human beings. The typification of human beings is, therefore, analogous to token-identification. What is faced is a proximate reality whose "rigor" depends on considerations beyond the scope of analytical or deductive techniques.

Although a type emerges out of focus on tokens, this type is regarded as an ideal, not in the sense of perfection, but rather in the sense of the non-real that is simultaneously recognized as limited but useful for the purpose of inquiry.[14] It approximates reality sufficiently for the purpose of interpreting and understanding reality, but never as the sum-total of reality:

To examine typification and ideal typification, we return to the work of Max Weber. In one of his various formulations, Weber writes:

> The constructed scheme, of course, only serves the purpose of offering an ideal typical means of orientation. It does not teach a philosophy of its own. The theoretically constructed types of conflicting "life orders" are merely intended to show that at certain points such and such internal conflicts are possible and "adequate." They are not intended to show that there is no stand-point from which the conflicts could not be held to be resolved in a higher synthesis. As will readily be seen, the individual spheres of value are prepared with a rational consistency which is rarely found in reality. But they *can* appear thus in reality and in histor-ically important ways, and they have. Such constructions make it possible to determine the typological locus of a historical phenomenon. They enable us to see if, in particular traits or in their total character, the phenomena approximate one of our constructions: to determine the degree of approximation of the historical phenomenon to the theoretically constructed type. To this extent, the construction is merely a technical aid which facil-itates a more lucid arrangement and terminology. Yet, under certain conditions, a construction might mean more. For the ratio-nality, in the sense of logical or teleological "consistency," of an intellectual-theoretical or practical-ethical attitude has and always has had power over man, however limited and unstable this power is and always has been in the face of other forces of histor-ical life.[15]

Weber here identifies a fundamental feature of the effort to study social reality. The theorist is faced with the problem of identifying social phenomena without reducing them solely to their singular identifications. He faces two dimensions of typification.

First is the problem of typification itself. For social reality to be placed under any schema of understanding, it must be placed under some condition of generalization; otherwise, the theorist would be stuck with unique cases that are merely conjoined with other unique cases under investigation.[16] For the cases even to be considered in relation to each other—that is, as cases of a "type"—calls for placing each under a consideration that exceeds the cases while paradoxically exemplifying the cases themselves. In short, the cases have to be recognized as cases of a *particular* (versus singular) phenomenon. For example, consider the difference between proper name identification and ordinary name identification. The proper name refers to a unique reality, whereas ordinary names refer to generalizable realities. Let P be an ordinary name. One can recognize P-prime as an instance of P. Sociality is purely in the realm of the latter realities. The cases of social phenomena are tokens of their recognized type.

Second, the theorist faces the problem of typifying without stereotyping. He faces problems of cogency or relevance. He has to show not only that a particular instance is a token of a phenomenon type, but also that it really relates to other tokens in a methodologically rigorous way. Each token must be able to stand in relation to other tokens as valid instances of the same type. The type, then, stands as a form of anonymity of tokens. It exemplifies its instances without being uniquely and solely one of them. It lacks a proper name. This move of typifying particular instances of social reality has interesting phenomenological significance.

It should be clear at this point that we are raising the question of essence. In our earlier instances of contrasting Husserl with Aristotle, we pointed out that whereas the latter equates essence with substance, the former does not. For Husserl, substance is relevant to a dimension of reality that has no place in phenomenological description. That is because phenomenological essence is an appeal to a thing-itself (a type), but not a thing-*in*-itself (a type of being). Thus, phenomenology can talk about essence without essentialism—essence, that is, without necessity nor presumed, rigid, ontological commitments beyond the reality of the world in which one lives. What this suggests, then, is that one can talk about the world in meaningful ways without committing oneself to the thesis that the world "must" continue to be as it is presently conceived. Whether it "must continue to be" as presently conceived is not relevant to its description. What is important is *that* it is presently conceived in such-and-such a way and the conception itself can be communicated reflectively both to oneself and to others.[17]

From these concerns, we now find ourselves returning to Fanon with an arsenal of conceptual tools. It becomes clear what Fanon is up to, for instance, when he declares in *Black Skin, White Masks* that "Many Negroes will not find themselves in what follows. This is equally true of many whites. But the fact that I feel a foreigner in the worlds of the schizophrenic or the sexual cripple in no way diminishes their reality. The attitudes that I propose to describe are real. I have encountered them innumerable times" (p. 12). Here Fanon is both alluding to the limiting constants of studying human beings and the anonymous features of a communicable reality. All of the "attitudes" that constitute the "they" who are encountered, all of these instances mark typical features of a society that militates against human affirmation. This typicality marks "facts" of a world which seize and pervert the very foundations of anonymous interaction that mark typically human encounters. This is the "fact" or real experience (*l'expérience vécue*) behind the fifth chapter of *Black Skin, White Masks*, "The Fact of Blackness," and it is what serves as that chapter's underlying theme.

"The Fact of Blackness" is not only the globalization of blackness (*Wherever he goes, the Negro remains a Negro*), but also the perversion of anonymity that it represents. Typical anonymity is marked by epistemological limitations on the relationship between self and Other. Returning to Natanson:

> Most of us must settle for knowing a much smaller number of people, for knowing *about* a larger circle of fellow-men, and for being aware of multitudes who are and who will remain anonymous. This is the normal state of affairs. And if it is "normal" that most individuals are anonymous to most other individuals, then it

is evident that anonymity is a standard feature of everyday life; anonymity is part of the structure of the social world. Before any predications of value are made about anonymity, it should be understood that anonymity is an invariant feature of an existence lived in the taken-for-granted terms of ordinary life. What is implied by this taken-for-grantedness is the reciprocity of anonymity: I am anonymous to most Others as most Others are anonymous to me. What seems compellingly obvious about this reciprocity is qualified by the essentially egological standpoint of the person who is quick to acknowledge that *Others* are largely anonymous to him. To paraphrase Tolstoi's Ivan Ilych, it seems *right* that Others (at large) should be anonymous, but as for *me*, that would be too terrible. Yet in the most neutral terms, I—as an ordinary person—recognize that the reciprocity of anonymity in the social world cannot be gainsaid. (p. 24)

Racism renders the individual anonymous even to himself. The very standpoint of consciousness, embodiment itself, is saturated with a strangeness that either locks the individual into the mechanism of things or sends him away and transforms him into an observer hovering over that very thing. Thus, to be seen in a racist way is an ironic way of *not being seen* through *being seen*. It is to be seen with overdetermined anonymity, which amounts, in effect, to invisibility. For to be seen in a typically human way is to be seen as a point of epistemological limitation; one's subjectivity is called upon as a point of meaning. One has to get, as it were, beyond the "surface": "Man is a *yes* that vibrates to cosmic harmonies" (*Black Skin, White Masks*, p. 8)—"As soon as I *desire* I am asking to be considered. I am not merely here-and-now, sealed into thingness. I am for somewhere else and for something else. I demand that notice be taken of my negating activity insofar as I pursue something other than life; insofar as I do battle for the creation of a human world—that is, of a world of reciprocal recognitions" (p. 218). The perversion of anonymity—overdetermination—seals off such affirmations. "Look, a Negro!" identifies, points out, but does not inquire beyond the sphere of limited points of subjectivity. The Negro—who is typically *any* Negro—is irrelevant to his own characterization. All is known. Enough has been said. And like his identifiers, the Negro finds himself facing the objective alienation of his embodiment *out there*.

Fanon offers a series of provocative phenomenological descriptions of authentic embodiment, which he regards as embodiment subject to "an atmosphere of certain uncertainty" (pp. 110–111), and alienated embodiment, which is a form of the individual's being regarded as completely known. Both of these interpretations are built upon leitmotifs of anonymity. Authentic embodiment comports with

> A slow composition of my *self* as a body in the middle of a spatial and temporal world—such seems to be the schema. It does not impose itself on me; it is, rather, a definitive structuring of the self and the world—definitive because it creates a real dialectic between my body and the world. (p. 111)

But alienated embodiment is saturated with an onto-Historical schema that seals away sociality. Observe:

> I sit down at the fire and I become aware of my uniform. I had not seen it. It is indeed ugly. I stop there, for who can tell me what beauty is?. . . I am given no chance. I am overdetermined from without. I am the slave not of the "idea" that others have of me but of my own appearance. I move slowly in the world, accustomed now to seek no longer for upheaval. I progress by crawling. And already I am being dissected under white eyes, the only real eyes. I am *fixed*. Having adjusted their microtomes, they objectively cut away slices of my reality. I am laid bare. . . . I slip into corners, and my long antennae pick up the catch-phrases strewn over the surface of things—nigger underwear smells of nigger—nigger teeth are white—nigger feet are big—the nigger's barrel chest—I slip into corners, I remain silent, I strive for anonymity, for invisibility. Look, I will accept the lot, as long as no one notices me! . . . It was always the Negro teacher, the Negro doctor; brittle as I was becoming, I shivered at the slightest pretext. (pp. 114–117)

> Yes, we are—we Negroes—backward, simple, free in our behavior. That is because for us the body is not something opposed to what you call the mind. We are in the world. And long live the

Gordon

couple, Man and Earth! Besides, our men of letters [negritude]
helped me to convince you; your white civilization overlooks
subtle riches and sensitivity. (pp. 126–127)

I was haunted by a galaxy of erosive stereotypes: the Negro's *sui
generis* odor . . . the Negro's *sui generis* good nature . . . the
Negro's *sui generis* gullibility. (p. 129)

I wanted to be typically Negro—it was no longer possible. I
wanted to be white—that was a joke. (p. 132)

Fanon's use of theriomorphic language isn't accidental. In most
of his studies of racism, he identifies the ascription of zoological
features to people who are objects of racial hatred. In *Black Skin, White
Masks:* "I have always been struck by the speed with which 'handsome
young Negro' turns into 'young colt' or 'stallion'" (p. 167); In *A
Dying Colonialism:* "In the [European's] dream [of raping Algerian
women], the woman-victim screams, struggles like a doe, and as she
weakens and faints, is penetrated, martyrized, ripped apart" (p. 46); In
The Wretched of the Earth: ". . . the terms the settler uses when he
mentions the native are zoological terms. He speaks of the yellow
man's reptilian motions. of the stink of the native quarter, of breeding
swarms, of foulness, of spawn, of gesticulations. When the settler seeks
to describe the native fully in exact terms he constantly refers to the
bestiary. . . . Those hordes of vital statistics, those hysterical masses,
those faces bereft of all humanity, those distended bodies which are
like nothing on earth, that mob without beginning or end, those children who seem to belong to nobody, that laziness stretched out in the
sun, that vegetative rhythm of life. . . ." (pp. 42–43)

It has become apparent here that Fanon's phenomenology of
racism is also a phenomenology of colonialism, especially since colonialism has served as a leitmotif throughout our discussion of racism.
This consequence is due primarily to the context of Fanon's analysis
of racism. It is simply a fact of European colonialism that it places
greater stock in Europeans—in plain, *whites*—over people colonized
by Europeans. One might wonder, however, about cases in which

racism was not a feature of the conquering group. Fanon's response is that such a case wouldn't be a colonial one. Recall:

> It must in any case be remembered that a colonized people is not only simply a dominated people. Under the German occupation the French remained men; under the French occupation, the Germans remained men. In Algeria there is not simply the domination but the decision to the letter not to occupy anything more than the sum total of the land. The Algerians, the veiled women, the palm trees and the camels make up the landscape, the *natural* background to the human presence of the French. (*The Wretched of the Earth*, p. 250)

One can object that it is difficult to dominate any group of individuals without dehumanizing them in some way, and hence placing them on the level of a subhuman species. I think Fanon would agree with this. His point, however, is that the dynamics of domination are far more complex when applied to people who are recognized *as people* in the act of domination. The sadist, for instance, is aware of the humanity of his sex partner. It is understood that his domination will go only so far, although his pleasure rests on the threatening *possibility* of his going farther. There are limits. Thus, a conquering group that simply regards itself as conquering other human beings affords the conquered group a place for anonymity. For example, it wasn't the case in occupied France that every Frenchman was "guilty" of being French. Whereas in occupied China, every Chinese was suspect; in occupied India, every Indian was suspect; and in occupied America, every Native American was suspect, for each native was ultimately guilty of continued existence.

Fanon has received a great deal of criticism for the supposed crudeness of his description of colonialism and his supposed caricaturing of colonizers and colonized people, primarily due to his propaganda commitments.[18] These rejections are usually rooted in either theoretical models of cultural criticism, or models of classical Marxist, industrial-class struggles. There is, however, a general failure, on the part of such rejections, to appreciate the role of Fanon's phenomenological

commitments in his response to colonialism.[19] Although we may talk
of local narratives, texts, tradition, internal critics, prophetic thought,
and the proletariat, we do not find, from any of these standpoints, when
geared against Fanon, any attention being paid to Fanon's priority on
the everyday, the ordinary, the "normal." Had this been done, it would
have become immediately apparent that Fanon's descriptions of colonialism are premised upon the thesis that colonialism, phenomenolog-
ically understood, is a presentation of the extraordinary as the ordinary,
the abnormal as the normal, the pathological as the logical, the inhu-
mane as the humane. In this regard, his descriptions appear exaggerated
by virtue of the degree to which we have been desensitized to the loot-
ing that represents colonization and neocolonization, where "wealth is
not the fruit of labor but the result of organized, protected robbery"
(*The Wretched of the Earth*, p. 191). We know that sometimes our call for
"complexity" masks our own efforts to "explain away," as Husserl said,
"under the pressure of prejudice what has been seen." Fanon attempts
to reintroduce the extraordinary back into the extraordinary.

It follows, then, that the response against colonialism which he
demands us to make is paralleled by the response he demands against
racism: that what is accepted as ordinary must be transformed; that the
everyday should be accessible to the once-colonized. But on the question of going from a circumstance of colonialism to *post*colonialism,
Fanon notes that the everyday cannot be the colonizer's everyday—
for even the colonizer's everyday is a form of false-reality. It is simply
bad faith to hide from one's role in oppression, or even from encouragement of oppression. Instead, the colonized must claim a world that
would constitute *his* or *her* normal, everyday, prosaic world.

How can this be done?

In *A Dying Colonialism*, Fanon's answer is resolute: the colonized
can achieve an authentic existence through revolutionary praxis.[20]
Fanon argues that the mundane features of an extraordinary circumstance, like revolutionary efforts toward decolonization, can transform
our consciousness of the *colonial* natural attitude, the colonial everyday
world, into its proper place of injustice, pathology, abnormality, and

misanthropy. The colonial natural attitude must be brought under reflection as an object of revolutionary transformation. Thus, like Paulo Freire, Fanon regards revolution as an edifying influence so long as it is "bottom-up"—in short, emerges from the experience of the colonized, or disenfranchised, or the oppressed.[21] Throughout the work, Fanon provides interpretive sociological descriptions of transformations of the meanings of certain behaviors in the phenomenological vein. For example, in his discussion of Algerian women, "Algeria Unveiled," he simultaneously offers a hermeneutic of the colonized people of Algeria through a phenomenology of the body. This phenomenological description explores the correlation of the "body"/individual Algerian woman with the Algerian "nation"/people. The European fantasies of raping Algerian women that we mentioned earlier are psychoanalytical projections of a political reality—the relation of colonizer to colonized, projections rich in psychoanalytical significance. The colonizer "penetrates" the colonized and plants seeds into "her" soil. In addition, she, the colonized, is expected to be grateful for such a "gift." She is expected to nurture it to "full term."

Our allusions to a sexually constructed consumption of dominated cultures aren't accidental. If we bracket the question of annexation from the point of view of the colonized, we will find a rich history in the European cultural-anthropological mores of power acquisition. For example, in her study on tragedy, Eva Figes makes the following observation,

> So how did Oedipus come to hold his high office? He was of course a *tyrannus* and not a hereditary monarch, and from what we know about kingship patterns, both in Greece and elsewhere, it is safe to assume that he became tyrannus by marrying the widow of his predecessor. There is an interesting suggestion, put forward by Frazer in his *Early History of Kingship*, that matrilineal descent may have persisted longer in royal families. There are innumerable examples in Greek mythology.[22]

Historically, one can acquire monarchical power through heredity or by marrying a queen. Alexander the Great's practice of marrying the princesses and queens of societies the Macedonians conquered is well known. What is of concern here is the role of these marriages as a means of legitimating the presence of a change of power that is not chosen by the people. Symbolically, the colonizer's presence calls for some form of legitimation. Although hosts of ideological rationalizations are often offered—for example, the advantages of "civilization"—there is still the question of symbolic acceptance. The conqueror stands as ruler *tyrannus*. He stands as the unchosen husband of the mother of the land. The relation of the conqueror to the conquered takes the agrarian form of matrimonial consummation. Algeria could not be completely conquered until she was unveiled:

> At an initial stage, there was a pure and simple adoption of the well-known formula, "Let's win over the women and the rest will follow." . . . This enabled the colonial administration to define a precise political doctrine: "If we want to destroy the structure of Algerian society, its capacity for resistance, we must first of all conquer the women; we must go and find them behind the veil where they hide themselves and in the houses where the men keep them out of sight." (*A Dying Colonialism*, pp. 37–38)

Fanon argues that the veil, regardless of its traditional function, is transformed under colonialism into a mark of resistance. The Algerian woman thus became the embodiment of cultural resistance *and* violation. During the period of revolutionary struggle, the veil goes through a dialectic between colonized signification, traditional Muslim signification, and its purely functional role as an opportune mode of concealment. Veiled women became an important means of transporting weapons at one stage of the struggle (because of their ability to conceal contraband under traditional garments), and unveiled, "Europeanized" Algerian women became an important means of getting past enemy lines (because of the enemy's perception of their European dress representing their taking the Europeans' side in the struggle). The consequence, argues Fanon, was the utilization of the Algerian woman in novel ways which led to novel Algerian women's conceptions of what it meant to be an Algerian woman.

We find a similar transformation on questions of technology. The radio, which represented a French disruption of Algerian values, with its broadcasting of both French secularism and Catholicism, is dramatically anthropomorphized by Algerian revolutionaries during the period of struggle into the "voice of Algeria." This consequence was necessitated by the anonymity radios afforded over the publicity of newspapers which used to be bought or delivered by revolutionaries with risk of exposure. Literally, against the French "voice" was pitted a Muslim "voice."

Similarly, colonial medicine, which for the most part was a racket run by fortune-hunting European settlers who were also physicians, gives way to revolutionary medicine, borne out of the revolutionary struggle, out of exigency. Whereas colonial medicine served as a source of legitimation for colonialism ("civilized" medicine) and an instrument of torture against the revolutionaries, revolutionary medicine aimed fundamentally at empowering the Algerian revolutionaries and hence the Algerian people.

Finally, Algeria's European minority, being compelled to choose, will find within its ranks those who will participate in the revolutionary struggle on the side of the Algerians, and through such an engagement they develop the new value of being an Algerian over being French. Since such praxis is fundamentally premised upon emancipation of Algerians, the Europeans—although facing the reality that the revolution is not for them—face what Fanon would identify as emancipation of the human being in Algeria. This occurs through the recognition of a justice that is no longer for Europeans but for those in whose way both Europe and Europeans once stood.

Fanon's text is far more complex than our brief discussion affords, and its faults are well known. Most prominent, in my view, is Fanon's presumption that a struggle for a revolutionary Algeria would be recognized and lived by the people as a struggle against colonialism instead of simply a struggle *against the French* or, worse, *all foreigners.* (In fairness to Fanon, these are features he accounts for in the third and fourth chapters of *The Wretched of the Earth.*) Be that as it may, even the xenophobic dimension of the people's struggle against the colonizers marks a significant change. It represents the placement of a limit on what may be presumed about colonized people. When such a limit is placed, there is a shift in the prosaic world. Inhabitants of that world are no longer "known" in their entirety; they become, even among themselves, unnervingly unpredictable.

Now it should be clear that Fanon's position on revolutionary struggle cannot be that of a panacea's relation to social ills. The very appeal to social panaceas of any sort reeks of bad faith. What the appeal to the everyday affords is an understanding of what is involved in building institutions that respond to the circumstances of oppressed people. Such institutions must afford a level of typicality that affords anonymity in the ordinary sense of human limitability. For Algeria, that should have meant that one could simply "be" a typical Algerian. In that typicality, there would be no presumption of an essential Algerian. In being a typical Algerian, one could live life amid the hubbub of everyday existence.

The pressing political question that follows is what kind of institutions encourage spaces of, and for, everyday life?

This is not the place in which to deal with such a question in detail. But we can consider this: a great deal of the contemporary world is enmeshed in a rather typical atypical condition—Life during war-time. In the midst of all this suffering, whether it be Haiti, Rwanda, former-Yugoslavia, Indonesia, or inner-cities of the United States of America, there are people who dream, as they go through day-to-day efforts at survival, for times in which one can settle for more than simply being alive.

FOUR

_____

Tragic Revolutionary Violence and Philosophical Anthropology

The objects the *imitator* represents are actions, with agents who are necessarily either good men or bad—the diversities of human character being nearly always derivative from this primary distinction, since the line between virtue and vice is one dividing the whole of mankind.

—Aristotle

We know that tragedy usually involved a "change from prosperity to adversity," as Aristotle put it, though for Aristotle the only reason for having a king as the protagonist was the fact that he had fortune and prosperity to lose. And yet we know that the welfare of a king involved the welfare of his people, so his misfortune or misconduct would appear to explain the misfortune of his people.

—Eva Figes

He only can understand the deep satisfaction which I experienced, who has himself repelled by force the bloody arm of slavery. I felt as I never felt before. It was a glorious resurrection, from the tomb of slavery, to the heaven of freedom. My long-crushed spirit rose, cowardice departed, bold defiance took its place; and I now resolved that, however long I might remain a slave in form, the day had passed forever when I could be a slave in fact. I did not hesitate to let it be known of me, that the white man who expected to succeed in whipping, must also succeed in killing me.

—Frederick Douglass

LTHOUGH WE have explored several dimensions of Fanon's philosophical thought, it is perhaps a testament of the degree to which an author can be entirely subsumed—perhaps, as Nietzsche once described it, *decadently so*—by a single element of his thought so that his significance as a thinker and a human being is blurred in the struggle and in, as Walter Benjamin might have put it, the garbage heap that constitutes intellectual history.[1] This has certainly been the case with Fanon with regard to his discussion of violence in *The Wretched of the Earth*. Although I do not consider that aspect of his thought to be the center of his philosophical concerns, it is common practice in Fanonian scholarship to say *something* on Fanon's theory of violence. Despite Fanon's corpus of over a thousand pages of writing, those seventy-one pages have functioned as a core concern for many commentators. We find even Hannah Arendt, one of Fanon's most noted critics, commenting that "It seems that only the book's first chapter, 'Concerning Violence,' has been widely read," and in this regard she is absolutely correct.[2] Given the discussion we've been having about problems of legitimacy and the dynamics of a racist world, we could surmise outright that the attention paid to this dimension of Fanon's thought may rest more on the political and cultural realities of racism and colonialism. Fanon, like Mao Tse Tung, Malcolm X, Huey Newton, Che Guevara, Fidel Castro, or Régis Debray, represented a frightening reality to a white world: people of color and people of developing nations who were willing to use violence in their struggle for freedom.

We find Fanon's views on violence in his early work, *Black Skin, White Masks*: "I do not carry innocence to the point of believing that appeals to reason or to respect for human dignity can alter reality. For the Negro who works on a sugar plantation in Le Robert, there is only one solution: to fight" (p. 224). The question of violence also emerges in his comparison of the French black and the American black:

The former slave needs a challenge to his humanity, he wants a conflict, a riot. But it is too late: The French Negro is doomed to bite himself and just to bite. I say "the French Negro," for the American Negro is cast in a different play. In the United States, the Negro battles and is battled. There are laws that, little by little, are invalidated under the Constitution. There are other laws that forbid certain forms of discrimination. And we can be sure that nothing is going to be given free. (p. 221)

The ontological appeal is immediately apparent. One cannot give an Other his freedom, only his liberty. We face here the first irony in the struggle for social change, for if one stands prostrate before the possibility of one's freedom, that freedom itself carries the resonance of a judgment to which only self-concealment or bad faith seems an ally:

But when one has taken cognizance of this situation, when one has understood it, one considers the job completed. How can one then be deaf to that voice rolling down the stages of history: "What matters is not to know the world but to change it." (p. 17)

In *The Wretched of the Earth*, Fanon achieves more than a rich presentation and virulent critique of colonial dynamics and neocolonialism. He also achieves a powerful testament on the problem referred to by Fredric Jameson as the problem of *mediation*: "How do we pass, in other words, from one level of social life to another, from the psychological to the social, indeed, from the social to the economic?" (*Marxism and Form*, p. xiv). In Jameson's dialectic, if we were to place freedom after each adjective, we would find that we move from psychological freedom to political-economic freedom. But can the mediation involved in a transition from colonialism to postcolonialism ever be nonviolent? Fanon's reply is both famous and infamous.

Fanon's response has suffered from a great deal of misunderstanding primarily because of a failure to understand the role of two particular phenomena in his thought. The first is his existential-phenomenological humanism. The second is the role of tragedy as a dramatic resource and anthropological signifier.

Colonialism is a tragic situation. The opening passage of Fanon's discussion of violence in *The Wretched of the Earth* presages Eva Figes's observations on tragedy from our epigraph:

> National liberation, national renaissance, the restoration of nationhood to the people, commonwealth: whatever may be the headings used or the new formulas introduced, decolonization is always a violent phenomenon. At whatever level we study it— relationships between individuals, new names for sports clubs, the human admixture at cocktail parties, in the police, on the directing boards of national or private banks—decolonization is quite simply the replacing of a certain "species" of men by another "species" of men. Without any period of transition, there is a total, complete, and absolute substitution. . . . Its unusual importance is that it constitutes, from the very first day, the mini-mum demands of the colonized. To tell the truth, the proof of success lies in a whole social structure being changed from the bottom up. The extraordinary importance of this change is that it is willed, called for, demanded. . . . But the possibility of this change is equally experienced in the form of a terrifying future in the consciousness of another "species" of men and women: the colonizers. (pp. 35–36)

Here, the tragic stage is set. Aristotle defines tragedy as: "the representation of an action that is serious and also, as having magni-tude, complete in itself; . . . with incidents arousing *pathos* and fear, wherewith to accomplish its *catharsis* of such emotions" (149b24–28, emphasis added).[3] In pathos, one suffers from and with another's suffering; and in identifying the achievement of catharsis, which in ancient times referred to the medicinal activity of purgation and cleansing, we arrive at the following observation. Tragedy presents actions to the community that elicit communal suffering. The tragic lesson is that setting things "right," thereby setting the community right, calls for violent intervention—horrible interventions. Tragedy addresses the terror of mediation. So does Fanon.

A dimension of Fanon's discussion of violence that has received much attention is the cathartic elements or cleansing force of violence in his two-stage theory of liberatory mediation. The oppressed, he claims, achieve psychological liberation, or cleansing, by violating the oppressor.[4] They are then free to go on with the more organized forms of violence, praxis, that are necessary for the building of a new, liberated society. It should be noted, however, that although Fanon advances this thesis, to see this aspect of his discussion as its crux would be a case of not seeing the forest for the trees. The objection that is most often raised against Fanon's argument, for instance, is that psychological release through violence on another human being doesn't necessarily create a psychological state conducive to a political one.

On the question of the relation of the psychological to the political, Figes observes a similar error in Freud's psychoanalytic treatment of tragedy.[5] She argues that as interesting as Freud's ruminations on tragedy as aesthetic expression of libidinous desire may be, they ultimately betray a limitation of classical psychoanalysis; they fail to account for the *audience's* role in tragic presentation and the irrelevance of the characters' apperception, whether conscious or subconscious, of their actions. On the other hand, we may take recourse to earlier theories of tragedy, like Hegel's, Schopenhauer's, and Nietzsche's. From the standpoint of our focus on actions, Hegel's thesis of conflicting Right is on target, since it focuses on *action*. In Sophocles's *Antigone*, for instance, tragedy emerges as King Creon's rightful condemnation of a traitor and his niece Antigone's rightful efforts to provide a proper burial for her brother, who, in spite of his act of treason, remained her brother in body and subsequently in spirit. A problem with Hegel's focus, however, is that it, too, fails fully to appreciate the point of audience, because for the Greek (and Elizabethan) audiences, there was a definite *right* that was to be exemplified by the characters in the drama.[6] Schopenhauer, on the other hand, presents tragedy as an indirect bringing to consciousness that which we attempt dearly to avoid—the crime of existence itself and

71

the irretrievable fall of the just and the innocent. In the first volume of *The World as Will and Idea*, he writes that in tragedy:

> The unspeakable pain, the wail of humanity, the triumph of evil, the scornful mastery of chance, and the irretrievable fall of the just and innocent, is here presented to us; and in this lies a significant hint of the nature of the world and of existence. It is the strife of will with itself, which here, completely unfolded at the highest grade of its objectivity, comes into fearful prominence.[7]

An effect of "fearful prominence" is the suspension of egoistic attachments: "The egoism which rests on [the phenomenal world] perishes with it, so that now the *motives* that were so powerful before have lost their might, and instead of them the complete knowledge of the nature of the world, which has a *quieting* effect on the will, produces resignation, the surrender not merely of life, but of the very will to live" (p. 327). The conclusion of resentment reemerges with great emphasis in the third volume: "What gives to all tragedy, in whatever form it may appear, the peculiar tendency towards the sublime is the awakening of the knowledge that the world—life—can afford us no true pleasure, and consequently is not worthy of our attachment. In this consists the tragic spirit: it therefore leads to resignation" (p. 213). In Schopenhauer we find, albeit through an analysis whose point of departure is the question of motives, a direct assessment of tragedy's impact on the audience. But his conclusion of quietude, resentment, and pessimism destroys the dynamism of tragedy as *human* and *political* presentations. Schopenhauer ultimately makes life itself tragic, which renders even the notion of a "fall" incoherent and the specific content of setting things right before the *community* problematic. Nihilism and pessimism are hardly tragedy's message, unless Schopenhauer's Will becomes a naturalized, ideological, proverbial "system" or life-world that no one can change. Our criticism of Hegel applies here in an ironic way, given Schopenhauer's well-known hatred of Hegel. The Greek audience would have recognized Schopenhauer's conclusion of resentment not as a *goal* of tragedy, but a condition for which tragedy is a remedy.

Nietzsche, on the other hand, deals both with what the audience recognizes and forgets, but in his case it is the *audience* at particular historical moments that is rendered problematic. He focuses on communal elements of song and dance and the role of the chorus in the evolution of tragedy, and he adds a twist on the Aristotelian theme of catharsis by opening up the question of the community's releasing vital energies in the tragic event.[8] But again, there are questions of right that need to be addressed beyond the scope of decadence (the Apollonian triumph of Socrates) and roles of song and dance (the celebration of Dionysus). Why do kings and queens fall? Nietzsche has explored answers to this question in works like *Will to Power* and *Beyond Good and Evil*. A conclusion that can be drawn from those works is that Nietzsche's conception of tragedy comes from the standpoint of the powerful, where, being boundless, it becomes difficult to see why they should be bound at all. They *are* the tragic rulers. The audience is therefore left with a false sense of right. In Nietzsche's account, the matter of right:

> ... which sounds so grandly edifying to certain politicians (as though the democratic Athenians had represented in the popular chorus the invariable moral law, always right in face of the passionate misdeeds and extravagances of kings) may have been suggested by a phrase in Aristotle, but this lofty notion can have had no influence whatever on the original formation of tragedy, whose purely religious origins would exclude not only the opposition between the people and their rulers but any kind of political or social context. (p. 47)

Thus, at a certain stage in the history of Greek tragedy, the people are offered "right," and therein lies tragedy's death "by suicide" through Euripidean/Socratic rationalism instead of Dionysian ecstacy (p. 69). In Nietzsche's favor, it is worth noting that Dionysus is, among other manifestations, the god of tragedy. Like Schopenhauer, however, Nietzsche's ancient audiences at first face resentment on the one hand and, on the other, what tragedy ultimately offers them is a moment's glimpse beyond their egoism that

73

in its physical manifestation is exemplified by the ecstasy of the crowd in celebration.⁹ The problem is that Nietzsche's celebrated call for a transvaluation of values rids tragic audiences of their historic role in the drama, which they never transcended, nor transvalued, for again the question of seeing things set right reemerges with full force. Even if ecstatic, musical and religious expression and experience were among the audiences' goals, they also stood as cathartic moments of specific political content—an individual of high stature whose actions, by virtue of his or her political place in the community, affected the entire community. This conclusion holds whether the individual is a king, a high priest, or a god.

Our reference to bearing rightness alludes to the etymological source of tragedy itself. From the Greek words *tragos* (meaning goat) and *ôidê* (meaning song), tragedy carries the burden of the proverbial burden-carrier itself: the scapegoat. As Figes notes:

> The origin of the word 'tragedy' is thought to lie in the Greek word for a goat, and though the ritual associations are obscure one inevitably thinks of the Israelite scapegoat, which Aron was required to send into the wilderness with the sins of the community on its back. The rituals of cleansing and atonement did in fact require two goats, the second one being sacrificed for a sin-offering. We know that animal sacrifices were made at the start of drama festivals in Athens, as at other important public gatherings, such as the political assembly. . . . Tragedy in the theatre is the sad story of a central protagonist who, either deliberately or by accident, offends against the most fundamental laws of his society, those laws which are so basic as to be considered divine. . . . In tragedy a community can see . . . the central protagonist who has polluted his environment, *bringing disruption on himself and the community within which he lives,* is eliminated, whereupon peace and order are restored. Whether that protagonist intended to break the divine social laws or not is beside the point. (pp. 11–12, emphasis added)

Returning to the *Antigone*, Creon is, for the Greek audience, a *flawed* king. But Antigone is also *flawed* by dint of origin. Like her brothers, she is the progeny of the unholy marriage of a flawed king to a flawed queen—Oedipus (whose name for ancient Greek audiences is recognizable as both knowing-foot and swollen-foot) and his mother, Jocasta.[10] All of these characters are oddly "set up" for suffering, for it is in fulfilling who they are, by virtue of their publicly recognized roles of power and communal responsibility; in fine, their characters, their strengths and their flaws, that they encounter what they must do. All of them bring calamity upon their community. For the community's demands to emerge, the kind of rightful action that must emerge is the reconstitution of justice. In other words, regardless of the characters' points of view, the world must be placed back into a certain order. The tragedy in tragedies is that the "innocence" of the characters who occupy a wrongful place in the drama is ultimately irrelevant. Thus, the tragic protagonist finds himself guilty by virtue of deed and circumstance, not intent, and finds himself suffering, ironically, for the sake of justice. The tragic drama cleanses the community of its own evasions. Justice is tragically restored.

But what about the modern scapegoats—aboriginal peoples, people of color (particularly "blacks"), Jews, Muslims, women, gays, the working- and under-classes, and so on?[11] The immediate response is that, in such cases, there is not tragedy but blatant injustice, for the burden of bearing the community's evils is placed upon the *powerless* instead of the powerful. In effect, the tragic stage has been turned upside down.[12] Thus, the revolutionary possibility of tragedy is that its object of degradation, if you will, is always the powerful. But the irony of tragedy is that it promises a form of restoration that can never truly be "as things were before." Tragedy is, fundamentally, in Sartrean language, progressive-regressive.

For Fanon, the oppressed confront the oppressor on multiple levels. On the situational level, an oppressed individual confronts the oppressor with an objective limitation of humanity. It is irrelevant what the colonized or oppressed individual may think of himself in relation to members of the colonizing or oppressing group. Everyday he confronts the objective reality of his life's inequality. His death will never rip through the overdetermined anonymity of nature-like existence. He looks around him at the slaughterhouse that constitutes, say, colored life in the modern and contemporary ages and he finds it difficult to distinguish colored life from the array of other animals that sink each day into the belly of consumption, death, and irrelevance. At times of trouble, it is the whites who are scurried off to safety; in the midst of thousands of colored deaths, it is the loss of an occasional white life that rips into the consciousness of the world—the world, in this case, usually coded as "free" or "civilized," which means, ultimately, European, Western, White. In the prisons, he sees colored captives, especially in cases where whites are victims of violent crimes, but rarely whites, and nearly never whites in cases where colored people are victims of white violent crimes. Eventually, it becomes important to equalize matters. If he cannot make a colonized or colored life as good as a white one, he can at least make a white one no more valuable than a colonized or colored one; he can, that is, bring the white god down to humanity. In the words of William Jones:

> . . . it is necessary to challenge [Dr. Martin Luther King, Jr.'s] familiar preachment that "an eye for an eye" philosophy is immoral because it would ultimately lead to a blind society. It might produce a one-eyed society, but not necessarily a blind one. In the situation where we each have only one eye, we may have the basis for the beginning of authentic inter-personal relations.[13]

Here we see the stages of a tragic story. For in its symbolic form, violence always takes the path of someone's being dragged "downward." The human being tragically emerges out of a violent situation of "gods" and the "wretched" in the violent.

At this point, it is necessary for us to explore some features of violence. We shall not spell out the many ways in which Fanon has used the word *violence*, since there is ample literature on that elsewhere.[14] Instead, we shall focus on a construction of violence that emerges from both the theories of human science and philosophical anthropology that we have advanced thus far.

Violence is fundamentally an activity that emerges from the categories of agency that we examined in our discussion of action; where there is no subjectivity, there is no violence. There has to be consciousness of an imposition that is not, or has not been, requested. In violence, or violation, there is a crossing of a threshold, there is the squeezing of options from the realm of choice. In this regard, violence is a relative intentional or situational phenomenon; there is a world of difference between simply slicing through another's chest with a sharp blade and committing surgery. What mediates the relativity of violent phenomena are both intentional apprehension of violent phenomena and contextual norms of justice and injustice that constitute the meanings of such phenomena. Thus, it is all the intentional features that transform behavior into action, constituting the surgeon's activity as surgery. And on the question of the normative assessment of violence, it is when violence is linked to the innocent that there is victimization, and when linked to the guilty, retribution.

But guilt and innocence are often blurred by the interests that dominate violent situations. Muggers who harm their victims often complain, for instance, that their victims "deserved" what happened to them because of their stupidity or their slow responses. Rapists often describe their victims as controlling the circumstances; in fact, they may even try to construct *themselves* as victims of female "enticements." Or consider cases of racism. The cry of white victimization from Affirmative Action in the United States has reached the point of becoming shrill. I have read columns by white students and faculty complaining of the victimization of white male opportunity at my home university, a place where there are forty thousand students, two thousand of whom are blacks, and where two thousand faculty members can boast of only seventeen blacks. As long as the justice of the *status quo* is presumed, *any* response that portends real change will take the form of violence.

For Fanon, colonialism is fundamentally a violent situation since the stage is set in motion between two kinds of interests—the interest of the colonizer and the interest of the colonized. From the standpoint of the colonizer, his place in the colony is not an unjust one. To replace him is to replace the innocent. For the colonized, his previous place in his society was not an unjust one. The fact that he has been replaced reflects an injustice. The former faces the threat of violence; the latter is already living it. The situation begins to take on tragic dimensions when the discourse on method—mediation—emerges with teleological import: ". . . the last shall be first."

There are uncomfortable dimensions to the problem which those in power will be unwilling to address—unwilling, ultimately, because they are used to having others' cake and eating it, too—and one of these dimensions is the legitimation crisis that we have raised at the outset: the very conditions that they may place upon the praxis of oppressed people may ultimately be conditions that will make no difference.[15] In his critique of one of the twentieth century's foremost proponents of nonviolence, William Jones identifies this phenomenon thus:

> Why this bewildering way of praising King? I must be frank—because of the exalted status white Americans have given him. Like the role assigned to Jesus, King has become the Black Messiah, the singular and exclusive pattern for blacks slavishly to imitate in their ethical models. Black leaders are indexed as militants or as violent, not on the basis of their actual thought and action, but by virtue of how far they stray from his footsteps. . . . King's dream has become a dreadful nightmare because whites have refused to act altruistically, all the while urging blacks to accept the nonviolent strategy, a strategy that is doomed to failure from the start because of white inactivity. Is there any wonder that blacks are suspicious of white glorification of the Black Messiah? . . . But perhaps the most compelling testimony of white America's unconscionable exploitation of King as a white guardian is the scandal of its response to his Viet Nam Policy. Whites incessantly praised his philosophy of nonviolence upon blacks—when faced with the other alternative of a Malcolm X—as the instrument for social, political, and economic change. Yet when King was consistent and advanced the same policy for Americans in Viet Nam, he was dropped like

a hot potato. This good for the goose (blacks) but not for the gander (whites) principle unwittingly displays the true status of King in the hearts and minds of white Americans. (pp. 233–234, 235, and 239 respectively)

The power of Malcolm X's position, Jones argues, is that he rejected Mao's (caricatured) "only the gun" rule and King's (simplified) "never the gun" rule and argued for a "don't rule out the gun" rule. The important issue in every struggle is the question of relevant action. One doesn't know in advance what will be most appropriate for the achievement of a people's goals, nor will one know their potentials, whether violent or not, in advance. Like Malcolm X, Fanon believes that struggle can take many forms, and its scariest one—armed resistance—should never be ruled out. In fact, it must be used for its impact of making the colonizer appreciate the gravity of the situation.

But against this backdrop is another Fanonian point that is implicit in Jones's distrust of white approval. If the oppressor or the colonizer perceives the very notion of a postcolonial society as a violent condition—because it displaces him—then his very call for a nonviolent solution amounts to the preservation of colonialism, or at least a transformation of colonialism into a condition that he will prefer, which amounts to a form of *neo*colonialism.

Fanon is right, in this regard. Nonviolent transformation of power boils down to none at all. Violence is broader than bullets, knives, and stones. Violence, fundamentally, is a form of taking that which has been or will not be willingly surrendered. Regardless of the perceived justice or injustice of the matter, regardless of the place of power in the matter, as long as someone is losing something that he currently has and wants to keep, there is violence.

Moreover, since oppression is ultimately an objectified reality supported by the precarious edifice of human reality, both actors, the oppressed and the oppressor, face a Catch-22 in the period of liberation. For just like the oppressed, when all is said and done, the oppressors are human beings. The tragic scapegoat who bears the burden of the sins of colonialism, then, is human being itself. In this regard, the oppressed and the oppressor converge as sufferers during the period of liberation. If the postcolonial, postracist world is to emerge, colonizers face the problem of its emerging through the resistance and eventual submission of colonizers and racists. The tragedy of the colonial and racist situation, then, is the price that has to be paid for the emergence of such a society. If the master's dirty values are accepted as a source of liberation, then no slave can be free without getting his hands dirty. But why must the colonized be "clean"?

We find in Fanon's treatment of violence, then, a rather powerful dimension of his philosophical anthropology. In *Black Skin, White Masks*, he portended this dimension through Jean-Jacques Rousseau's adage (which Fanon cites by way of Nietzsche) that the tragedy of the man is that he was once a child. The adult world carries the burden of godless freedom. It is a freedom without a mother or a father. In the midst of this freedom, humanity becomes the source of value. But the violence that emerges, first in the period of conquering one sector of humanity, and then in the period of that sector's efforts toward its emancipation, challenges the very core of human potential and self recognition. By the penultimate chapter of *The Wretched of the Earth*, Fanon draws out this dialectic through an examination of case studies of torturers and resistance-fighters. The torturer's violence pushes him directly into the face of human misery; the resistance-fighter's actions push him into the world of an irremediable fact. Even oppressors suffer. Both face an existential reality in the midst of which trembles the possibility of a human being. For despite the chains of command, despite the various decision-makers at play, what eventually afflicts both the torturer and the resistance-fighter is the sheer anonymity of The Enemy. The enemy who he has learned to hate is peculiarly absent from the shrieking flesh-and-blood reality in the torture chamber. The enemy who dominated Algeria seemed peculiarly absent from such flesh-and-blood realities as sipping coffee outside a café at the moment before the bomb's explosion shattered it to pieces (see p. 253). Perhaps the most disturbing example in this section of *The Wretched of the Earth* is the case of the two Arabic boys who killed their best white friend (pp. 270–272). Fanon writes of one of the boys that:

> He did not deny having killed either. Why had he killed? He did not reply to the question but asked me had I ever seen a European in prison. Had there ever been a European arrested and sent to prison after the murder of an Algerian? I replied that in fact I had never seen any Europeans in prison.

The tragedy faced by anyone seriously engaged in struggle against the institutional encouragement of dehumanization is that institutionalized dehumanization is fundamentally a state of war. In such a state, the ordinary anonymity of which we spoke earlier is saturated with a pathological consciousness that makes any feature of human beings beyond their typifications fall to the wayside. To see colonialism and racism clearly is to see that where such conceptions of reality reign, there is a shift in the presuppositions of justice and fairness that may have operated within traditional mores and folkways. In the tragic struggle between the cause of liberation and the cause of colonial preservation, there is the painful rationality of an adult philosophical anthropology. We say "adult" here because of our previous allusion to the tragic adult in every child. In a child's world, there is no room for tragedy because values in such a world are so serious that they pretend that they are what they are not. In the adult world, values take on an ironic veneer. In the adult world, there are places in which justice and fairness are no longer relevant concerns. Even if it is argued that it is *wrong* for certain violations to occur, in the adult world such an argument is irrelevant, ultimately, if there is no will to change the fact that they continue to occur. The colonized people's struggle for liberation should not, then, be treated as equal to the colonizers' violence. For in the accomplishment of the former's struggle is the possibility, fragile though it may be, of a world that is not, by dint of its very structure, violent. We find a historical version of this dimension of emancipatory violence in C.L.R. James's classic study, *The Black Jacobins*, which is worth a lengthy quote:

> The slaves destroyed tirelessly. . . . They knew that as long as these plantations stood their lot would be to labour on them until they dropped. The only thing was to destroy them. From their masters they had known rape, torture, degradation, and, at the slightest provocation, death. They returned in kind. For two centuries the higher civilization had shown them that power was used for wreaking your will on those whom you controlled. Now that they held power they did as they had been taught. In the frenzy of the first encounters they killed all, yet they spared the priests whom they feared and the surgeons who had been kind to them. They, whose women had undergone countless violations, violated all the women who fell into their hands, often on the bodies of their still bleeding husbands, fathers, and brothers. "Vengeance! Vengeance!" was their war-cry, and one of them carried a white child on a pike as a standard. And yet they were surprisingly moderate, then and afterwards, far more humane than their masters had been or would ever be to them. They did not maintain this revengeful spirit for long. The cruelties of property and privilege are always more ferocious than the revenges of poverty and oppression. For the one aims at perpetuating resented injustice, the other is merely a momentary passion soon appeased. As the revolution gained territory they spared many of the men, women, and children whom they surprised on plantations. To prisoners of war alone they remained merciless. They tore out their flesh with red-hot pincers, they roasted them on slow fires, they sawed a carpenter between two of his boards. Yet in all the records of that time there is no single instance of such fiendish tortures as burying white men up to the neck and smearing the holes in their faces to attract insects, or blowing them up with gun-powder [from the anus], or any of the thousand and one bestialities to which they had been [routinely] subjected. Compared with what their masters had done to them in cold blood, what they did was negligible, and they were spurred on by the ferocity with which the whites in Le Cap treated all slave prisoners who fell into their hands.[16]

In a note after the phrase, "they were surprisingly moderate," James writes, "This statement has been criticised. I stand by it." One wonders who these critics were in terms of the audience they signified. When writers like James and Fanon write on revolution, the cathartic effect sought is from the audience for whom these texts are ultimately designed. Although the powerful is "seen," made apparent through being laid bare by texts like *The Black Jacobins* and *The Wretched of the Earth*, there is a form of violence that is played out to cleanse the readers just as ancient drama cleansed its audiences through the pathos of the powerful. But there is an ironic twist to the stage that is set by the revolutionary writer. Unlike the theater in which an audience sits for dramatic edification, there is no exit awaiting revolutionary subjects beyond their resolute awareness, reflection, and decision to create one. *The Wretched of the Earth* stands to the oppressed reader as a tragic text about a tragic world.

As an addendum to the formulation of violence in *The Wretched of the Earth* stands the ironic place of tragedy in the drama. For it is only human beings who are capable of tragedy, and in the unfolding of a tragic version of a particular, institutionalized version of human reality is the accountability of human beings who maintain structures that militate against human *being*. In effect, then, Fanon's theory of violence—in both its cathartic and organizing forms—is connected to his critical anthropology in a provocative way: it reveals the implications of a humanity that attempts to evade the challenge and responsibility of growing up.

FIVE

Fanon's Continued Relevance

If you respected
goodness or truth,
your awkward words
wouldn't be forced,
shame wouldn't sulk
in your eyes
and you'd tell me
what you really want.
—Sappho

A T THIS POINT, we come to the close of our discussion of Fanon with some considerations of his continued relevance.[1] Hussein Bulhan observes that there are, for instance:

a Frantz Fanon Center in Milan, Italy, and another in Lagos, Nigeria; a Fanon Research and Development Center and a Fanon School in Los Angeles, California; a Fanon Institute of Research and Training in Boston, Massachusetts; and a Frantz Fanon Collection at the Countway Library of Harvard University. During the Ben Bella regime in Algeria, a literary prize was also named for Frantz Fanon. For the past several years, a series of conferences honoring Fanon have been held in Atlanta, Georgia; Port-of-Spain, Trinidad; Mogadishu, Somalia; and Belaggio, Italy. More recently, when for the first time it became permissible to organize an international memorial of Frantz Fanon in his home island of Martinique following the emergence of a socialist and more tolerant regime in France, the participants included representatives from the Caribbean, Latin America, North America, Africa, Europe, and Asia. A year later, an international conference honoring Fanon was held in Hamburg, West Germany. Such wide recognition of a man who died at so early an age, and well over 20 years ago, underscores the stature of Fanon and the continued relevance of his ideas to a diverse international community. (p. 6)

In one sense, Fanon's relevance also continues in the mere fact that this book has been written and is being read. But there is a more substantial sense in which he is relevant to the current, and perhaps future, times by virtue of the richness of the challenges he has issued to his contemporaries and his present successors.

We have argued that Fanon embodies a crisis in the very effort to study and forge a better world for human beings. The crisis itself has been articulated as a form of bad faith, in which the ability to construct a *tomorrow* is concealed in a totalization of the present. But unlike his European contemporaries, Fanon saw this stagnation as an opportune moment, precisely because its ossification solidified the demand and praxis geared toward *new* concepts and a new humanity.

This question of humanity led us to a discussion of the existential dimension of the call for a radical approach to the study of human being. A consequence of this move is the rejection of human nature, but not a rejection of human responsibility and human interpretability. Our latter affirmations led to the view that an existentially situated history holds the key to the liberatory concerns with which Fanon was engaged. But this existential move does not entail a rejection of institutional or structural reality. The disembodied, asocial individual is a fantasy just as much as the corporeal, mechanistic, purely structural object of study is a fantasy. Both evince forms of bad faith. Instead, our philosophical departure led to a search for the possibility of human being, as an interpreted and interpreting reality, in the realm of the everyday, where the facets of anonymity reign with constant—though ultimately fragile—vibrancy. There, Fanon showed how institutional power squeezes anonymity into a perverse transformation of the social world into a dehumanizing one. In Fanon's explorations of the everyday, there are both a description and a prescription for a human and humane world.

Perhaps the most apparent testament to his continued relevance, however, is the growing body of post-Cold War literature on Fanon. Since our focus is on his contribution to the human sciences, we shall now focus on how this body of literature has addressed Fanon's treatment of one particular aspect of human phenomena—the phenomenon of oppression. I have also chosen this focus because of its popularity and controversy, sparked by one critic in particular—namely, Henry Louis Gates, Jr.—with his article, "Critical Fanonism."

Gates begins his discussion with a Lyotardian admonition against "global theory":

> One of the signal developments in contemporary criticism over the past several years has been the ascendancy of the colonial paradigm. In conjunction with this new turn, Frantz Fanon has now been reinstated as a global theorist, and not simply by those engaged in Third World or subaltern studies. (p. 457) [2]

Gates then declares his project, which is to show that the many
different Fanons represented by some commentators—conspicuously
determined by Gates's orbit of cultural studies' elite—reflect a limitation of the project of what Gates calls a "unified field theory of
oppression." He cites Edward Said's "Representing the Colonized:
Anthropology's Interlocutors" as an example of the kind of work in
which "Fanon as global theorist has been produced" (p. 459).[3] Gates
then runs through an itinerary of theorists, most of whom are "postmodern." His focus on the postmoderns is not only informed by their
eminence in his own area of cultural studies, but also because, as he
puts it, "Fanon's current *fascination* for us has something to do with the
convergence of the problematic of colonialism with that of subject-
formation. As a psychoanalyst of culture, as a champion of the
wretched of the earth, he is an almost irresistible figure for a criticism
that sees itself as both oppositional and postmodern" (p. 458, emphasis added). One wonders who might constitute the *us* whose response
to a thinker like Fanon is merely that of "fascination."

After pointing out the various tensions in the instances he
offers—Homi K. Bhabha's Fanon, who is rewritten as a postructural-
ist and a "black Lacan"; Abdul R. JanMohamed's Fanon, who maintains the resonance of alterity; Benita Parry's Fanon, who maintains
the provisional dimensions of liberating praxis; Gyatri Spivak's Fanon,
who ultimately speaks a colonial discourse because all discourse is
ultimately colonial; Albert Memmi's Fanon, who was a "European
Interloper," an alien to the "actual Third World," a Martinican ex
patriot, and a French linguistic snob—he concludes:

> Do we still need global, imperial theory—in this case, a grand
> unified theory of oppression; or, indeed, even the whole univer-
> salizing model of Theory that it presupposes; or, indeed, even the
> whole universalizing model of and an exclusive lien on the last
> word? It's no longer any scandal that our own theoretical reflec-
> tions must be as provisional, reactive, and local as the texts we
> reflect upon. Of course, discarding the imperial agenda of global
> theory also means not having to choose *between* Spivak and

Said, Greenblatt, Pease, or Jameson, Bhabha or JanMohamed or
Parry, even Fanon or Memmi; or, rather, it means not representing
the choice as simply one of epistemic hygiene. And it requires a
recognition that we, too, just as much as Fanon, may be fated to
rehearse the agonisms of a culture that may never earn the title
*post*colonial. (p. 470)

Against Gates's essay stands Cedric Robinson's "The
Appropriation of Frantz Fanon." Robinson correctly identifies the
Gates adherents' treatment of Fanon as part of their "self-referential
debates on colonial discourse" (p. 78). His aim is "to re-centre Fanon in
the current fashion of Fanon Studies." Robinson's choice of the
term—*re-centre*—is a response to the postmodern/poststructural
predilections of Gates's effort, which is, in effect, an effort at *de-centering*
Fanon in colonial and postcolonial studies. Robinson then advances
two points: "first, that Fanon in his revolutionary work mistook a racial
subject for his own class—those he termed the 'nationalist bourgeoisie';
and, secondly, of late, other representatives of that class have sought
selectively to reappropriate and apportion Fanon for a post- or anti-
revolutionary class-specific initiative" (p. 80). He proceeds to cite
examples of Fanon's supposed focus on petit-bourgeois elements of
black and colonized society and takes as literal those passages in Fanon's
oeuvre that are, to my understanding, sarcastic. It is as if Robinson hypo-
statized Fanon as a humorless intellectual.[4] He then sets up the standard
division between the young and the "mature" Fanon in terms of the
supposedly naïve *Black Skin, White Masks* and the prescient *The Wretched
of the Earth*. We find a similar divide among some Sartre scholars in
their views of *Being and Nothingness* (or for that matter, *Anti-Semite and
Jew*) and *Critique of Dialectical Reason*. In Marxist terms, the former kinds
of text represent concerns with bourgeois liberty and freedom, and the
latter with a more politically experienced form of praxis and revolutionary awareness, namely, Marxism. Then, after some discussion of the
obfuscating, alienating language of commentators like Bhabha and
Spivak, and their ultimate alienation from working- and underclass
people of color, Robinson shifts to the stance of candor:

But let us be frank. Though Fanon is the signifier, the immediate objects of Gates and his fellow anti-Fanonists (Bhabha and Spivak) are Edward Said, Abdul JanMohamed and Benita Parry. After all, Fanon is dead. But what threat, what offence are attached to Said, Parry and JanMohamed by the anti-Fanonists? What links Said, JanMohamed and Parry, if not Fanon, or merely Fanon? . . . We can only speculate on the sources of the misdirection and concealment. Remember Said and Parry both are aggressive advocates of global theory and liberation. The one Palestinian and the other South African, they have each spent much of their lives involved in liberation movements, and into merely those which are their "own." . . . What Said, JanMohamed and Parry now represent, and what Fanon once embodied, is the sustained attempt to locate and subsequently advertise a fixed and stable site of radical liberationist criticism and creativity. Little of this project survives in a literature which posits a psycho-existential complicity between the colonised and the colonisers, which spatially and temporally domesticates all social theory, and whose mechanics recognise no voice more authentic than their own. (pp. 87–88)

So we find ourselves with a class–critique of the sedimentation and bad-faith dimension of the crisis to which we have been referring:

Gates and his collaborators preserve and consume Fanon all in the same moment. . . . It seems more and more apparent that a metropolitan elite, whose domination and rule are increasingly disoriented by racialism, cannot hope to achieve a stable world order conspiring with a frenetic petit-bourgeois elite in the Third World. (pp. 88–89)

Robinson's criticisms remind me of an observation on the élite in capitalist and in Third World societies, a criticism which was also ironically made by Sartre:

Thus the bourgeois makes himself a bourgeois by denying that there are any classes, just as the worker makes himself a worker by asserting that classes exist and by realizing through his revolutionary activity his "being-in-a-class." *Being and Nothingness* (p. 680) [5]

The second observation was made by C. L. R. James:

We must see Fanon as the political activist and writer who is saying that now we have actually achieved independence we have to fight against not only the old imperialism creeping back: we have to carry on a desperate all-out struggle against those native leaders who may have fought for independence. Many do not represent the forward movement of the underdeveloped peoples to some new stage of economic and political progress. Says Fanon: after independence those become the enemy.[6]

At this point, how do we assess this Gates–Robinson exchange that we have occasioned (since these two articles were published in separate journals with apparently no direct dialogue between the two).

Well, first, since our concerns are primarily in the areas of crisis and human science, the specific dynamics of literature and Marxism applied to colonialism need to be considered in light of the degree to which they manifest themselves in our thesis. If we consider Robinson as the type of theorist whom Gates's criticisms are geared against, we find, in each criticism of the other's *type*, two manifestations of bad faith: in Gates, the self-evasive transcendency of theoretical skepticism; and in Robinson, the self-evasive security of the serious man. (Whether both theorists are *actually* serious men in bad faith is beside the point here, since, given our analysis of anonymity, such a construction (rigid and permanent) is destined to fail. It is simply in *these* manifestations—these articles—that we find a problematic self-construction.) We are reminded of Fanon's injunction: "It is necessary to analyze, patiently and lucidly, each one of the reactions of the colonized, and every time we do not understand, we must tell ourselves that we are at the heart of the drama—that of the impossibility of finding a meeting ground in any colonial situation." (*A Dying Colonialism*, p. 125)

We will begin with Robinson, since I am admittedly sympathetic with Robinson's views of the postmodern and anti-Fanonians' positions, but not with his views of Fanon. I have already pointed out that Robinson's article suffers the flaw of assuming a humorless

Fanon.[7] But more, some of Robinson's assertions are blatantly false. For example, the assertion that Fanon limits his analyses to petit-bourgeois elements of colonial society is clearly false by virtue of the fact that throughout his corpus, the *fellah* and the peasant play central roles, roles that are emphasized even to the point of even being considered, in the eyes of some commentators, valorized.[8] Here is an early example from Fanon's first major work:

> For the moment, let us go to welcome one of those [blacks who have fled to Paris and] who are [now] coming home. The "newcomer" reveals himself at once; he answers only in French, and often he no longer understands Creole. There is a relevant illustration in folklore. After several months of living in France, a country boy returns to his family. Noticing a farm implement, he asks his father, an old don't-pull-that-kind-of-thing-on-me peasant, "Tell me, what does one call that apparatus?" His father replies by dropping the tool on the boy's feet, and the amnesia vanishes. Remarkable therapy. *Black Skin, White Masks* (pp. 23–24)

Examples like this are found throughout the Fanonian corpus. The other flaw from which Robinson's response suffers is its very limited conception of an existential dimension in liberation theory. Robinson writes as though an existential turn is an anti-Marxist one, and he makes the additional error of linking such a turn to a form of naïve psychologizing. As Bulhan points out:

> [T]hose who often wrote on Fanon were political scientists, historians, or sociologists. Naturally, they approached his works according to the priorities, orientation, and concepts of their disciplines. Most of them deliberately de-emphasized his psychological contributions. In fact, Woddis and Nghe went so far as to regret the psychological component of his sociopolitical analysis. Having mistakenly reduced his psychology to "existentialism" they used this supposedly negative label to discredit his genuine differences with orthodox Marxism. (p. 7)

In the United States, existentialism is invariably confused with libertarianism. It was my task in addressing the philosophy of existence to chart not only what philosophy of existence may have meant for Fanon, but also to show the distinction between Fanonian existential phenomenology and Fanonian psychology. The former includes elements of the latter, but it is an error to reduce one to the other, especially since some of the concerns of the philosophy of existence are the very conditions in which a science of psychology can exist at all. As for Marxism, it should be noted that Fanon's philosophy of the human sciences compelled him not to regard even Marxism as a closed system of thought. Renate Zahar has shown, for example, that although Fanon was more in line with Marxist-Leninism, his contribution was more as an innovator, not a disciple. Fanon's focus on intellectual alienation was not spurred on by petit-bourgeois predilections, as Robinson suggests, but rather, an understanding of what constituted uncovered domain. Fanon has shown that reciprocal recognition, an assumption needed for an identity-relation between the colored working class and the white working class, was absent.[9] The consequence was that:

> While the American Negroes are already engaged in fighting for their freedom, the Africans [at the time of *Black Skin, White Masks*], oppressed by colonialism, have not yet seized this opportunity. . . . The question is, however, whether the same does not likewise apply to European conditions and whether Hegel's dialectical turn is not only an idealistic one. Neither did the bourgeoisie in its struggle for emancipation succeed in freeing itself entirely from feudal structures—in Germany, if not in other countries, its basic aspirations for self-realization were not so much aimed at constituting a class of its own as at being admitted to the social sphere of the nobility—nor did the proletariat succeed in its emancipation as the working class. There was no revolution. This digression may have helped to throw light on the question why Fanon attached such great importance to detecting the mechanisms of alienation, and which were the *praxis*-oriented political intentions informing the theory he elaborated. (Zahar, *Frantz Fanon*, pp. 16–17)

Bulhan is less kind. "I consider the debate on race versus class a digression," he declares, "when the black middle class argues for the primacy of 'race' to mask its historical complicity with oppression or when traditional Marxists minimize the significance of 'race' to underplay the crimes of Europe and its descendants against people of color" (p. 13).

Again, we find the key concern of *relevance* emerging. And to get at what is relevant, what is appropriate, requires, as we have seen in our discussion of action, an understanding of the *purpose* of the action (which can be construed as theory or practice) under consideration. The radical reflective credo of apperceptive critique finds support here.

Let us now address Gates's treatment of Fanonism, which he regards as an effort at a grand, unified, field theory of oppression. But before addressing the theoretical flaws in his position, I should like to point out some factual errors in Gates's effort to discredit Fanon's liberatory significance. Appealing to Memmi, Gates writes that Fanon:

> . . . is, indeed, a far more harried subject, a central fact of whose life is his dislocation from the "actual Third World." Of course, we know from his biographers and from his own account that Fanon, whose mother was of Alsatian descent, grew up in Martinique thinking of himself as white and French: and that his painful reconstitution as a black West Indian occurred only when he arrived at the French capital. Yet at this point—again, in Memmi's narrative—Fanon loses himself as a black Martinican: . . . indeed, he "never again set foot in Martinique." Yet his attempts to identify himself as an Algerian proved equally doomed. As Fanon's biographers remind us, most Algerian revolutionaries scant his role and remain irritated by the attention paid to him in the West as a figure in Algerian decolonization: to them—and how ironic this is to his Western admirers—he remained a European interloper. (p. 468)

One wonders which Algerians are both Memmi and Gates referring to. It certainly isn't the ones who instituted a Boulevard

Frantz Fanon, a Frantz Fanon Hospital, and a Frantz Fanon High School in Algeria. Nor is it siginificant that Fanon's mother was of Alsatian descent. On the matter of Fanon's "lineage," Richard Onwuanibe has written the following:

> Frantz's father drew from mixed Indian-Martinique blood. He was a government official and a freemason. Frantz's mother, an illegitimate daughter of mixed parents, had Alsatian blood in her ancestry.[10]

Both his parents were of African descent, and sufficiently so for the consequence of their children attending a segregated black lycée (ibid). Fanon was, in short, a man of color, and the Fanon family, a working family of eight children and never poor, was a black family (Bulhan, p. 16). But even with Fanon's grandfather being a white Frenchman, it is a well-known constant in the sociology of race and racism that such a family would have been regarded as a "colored family," if not specifically a black one. Fanon's childhood experiences show that he had no reason to think of his family as being, under the segregated conditions they faced, anything other than a black one.

In regard to the fact that Fanon did not settle in Martinique after passing the *Médicat des hôpitaux psychiatriques,* I don't know what to make of either Memmi's or Gates's innuendo. Both Hansen (p. 38) and Bulhan (pp. 30–33) point out that Fanon wanted to go to Senegal to work under Leopold Senghor, whom he had admired at that time because of Senghor's history with *Présence Africaine* and the development of negritude in the 1940s.[11] Senghor never responded, so Fanon took the only offer he received for a position in Africa, namely the post at Blida-Joinville Hospital in Algiers. It is also well-known that Fanon had hoped to become Algeria's representative in Cuba, which would have placed him back into the Caribbean. In fact, when he attended the Second Congress of Black Writers, which was held in 1959, he spoke as a member of the Antillean delegation, which hardly reflected a desire not to be identified with the place from which he came. But all this is beside the point. Fanon was dead within eight years of taking his post in Algiers. He was already caught up in the Algerian liberation struggle within two years of being there. That struggle occupied the rest of his short life, the remainder of which he also spent on the assassination lists of right-wing French groups. It is unclear why he should be condemned for not going "home," especially since, at that time, death certainly awaited him there in light of Martinique's affirmation of its status as a French possession. The spectacle is recounted by Caute:

> Malraux, former left-wing novelist and hero of the Spanish Civil War and now a Minister of the Fifth Republic, was dispatched by de Gaulle to secure the umbilical cord which tied the Antilles and Guiana to France. This was the Malraux whose concepts of Western man and Western civilization Fanon sarcastically derided. Malraux traveled from village to village, receiving flowers and laying them at the foot of the bust of the Republic or, when she was not available, on the ubiquitous plaques commemorating Schoelcher, the enemy of slavery. At Fort-de-France, the mayor of the town, none other than Aimé Césaire, received Malraux with the words, "I salute in your person the great French nation to which we are passionately attached." ...Then the crowd took up the *Marseillaise*. And here Malraux, with his unique, rhapsodical bastardization of left-wing and right-wing metaphors, mocks what Fanon stood for ... "It was," says Malraux, "the cry of black liberty, that of Toussaint l'Ouverture's fighters and of the eternal Jacquerie—inextricably mixed with revolutionary hope and physical fraternity" (Caute, pp. 61–62).[12]

Moreover, the reference to Fanon's use of a translator in Algeria is rather misguided since (1) even native Algerians spoke French and (2) there are countless instances of Fanon's references to Arabic terms in his texts. In *Black Skin, White Masks* and *Toward the African Revolution*, Fanon even remarks how the French he spoke was always understood by his patients, and how he refused to patronize them with what he called pidgin and childlike speech. In fact, he was vehement:

> If a man who speaks pidgin to a man of color or an Arab does not see anything wrong or evil in such behavior, it is because he has never stopped to think. I myself have been aware, in talking

to certain patients, of the exact instant at which I began to slip. . . . Examining this seventy-three-year-old farm woman whose mind was never strong and who is now far gone in dementia, I am suddenly aware of the collapse of the *antennae* with which I touch and through which I am touched; . . . the fact that I condescend to her in my quest for a diagnosis, are the stigmata of a dereliction in my relations with other people. What an idealist, people will say. Not at all: It is just that the others are scum. I make it a point always to talk to the so-called *bicots* in normal French, and I have always been understood. They answer me as well as their varying means permit; but I will not allow myself to resort to paternalistic "understanding." (*Black Skin, White Masks*, pp. 32–33)

Fanon's candor here stands opposed to the form of thinking on the politics of language that became fashionable during the 1970s and 1980s in the USA and Britain. He refuses to be anyone's signifying "monkey." This is not to say that Fanon calls for the elimination of the many creative variations on the European languages used by people of color. Fanon's view is most probably that the resources of language are broader than the political-economic order allows; but one must be careful about decontextualizing how power manipulates the various ways resources of language are deployed and employed. In his insistence on the use of the formal *vous* during interviews with Arab patients, Fanon stretches this point with a recognition of hierarchies that are certainly not postmodern:

There is one thing that might give food for thought. Speaking to an Arab, the student or the doctor is inclined to use the second person singular. It's a nice thing to do, we are told . . . to put them at ease . . . they're used to it . . . I am sorry, but I find myself incapable of analyzing this phenomenon without departing from the objective attitude to which I have constrained myself. "I can't help it," an intern once told me, "I can't talk to them in the same way that I talk to other patients." Yes, to be sure: "I can't help it." If you only knew the things in my life that I can't help. If you only knew the things in my life that plague me during the hours when others are benumbing their brains. If you only knew . . . but you will never know. (*Toward the African Revolution*, p. 9)

Then there is the matter of Fanon's supposedly being seen as a "European interloper" by the Algerians. This is the type of reasoning behind some African Americans' delusion of their being seen in the world as Americans first, or those in the Francophone Caribbean who think they are seen as either French or Caribbean first, and perhaps those in Europe who think they are seen as European first. While presenting the first two chapters of this volume in the Czech Republic, I had the opportunity to travel through both Western and Eastern Europe. Throughout, I was identified—whether positively or negatively—as African. I took it as a coded version of *black*. If there is a distinction between being black and being white among Arabs, I don't see any reason why there would have been any difference for Fanon, and in fact there wasn't any. In his own words:

> Some ten years ago I was astonished to learn that North Africans despised men of colour. It was absolutely impossible for me to make any contact with the local population. (*Black Skin, White Masks*, p. 102)

Fanon makes this admission after documenting how antiblack racism manifests itself among Arabs, even those who were also regarded as blacks, in Africa. He also identified this phenomenon among blacks south of the Sahara. But the important point to remember here is that Arabs and North Africans are defined, in the racial constructions of nationalities that dominate the Euro-world, as Caucasian. Whether they are treated so in practice is another matter. For it can be argued that some of them are, in practice, "colored" Caucasians—that is, not "white" whites—and others are "honorary" whites, that is, "white Negroes." Hansen adds, "His luck was to be better in the future. It is interesting to note that Fanon did not react to Arab racism in the same way as he did to European racism. In a way he tended to think that Arab racism was part of the superstructure, a reflection of colonial racism occasioned by the colonial experience. He viewed it in the same terms in which he viewed Martinican expression of racist attitudes towards Africans" (p. 26). Recall that in

Fanon's essay, "West Indians and Africans," this expression of racism amounted to the view that in Africa, one finds the "blackest" blacks.

Finally, there is the problem not only of Gates's failure to provide much-needed contexts for his Fanon quotes, but also of his neglect of the proper context for the theorists he has chosen: namely, how they relate to other theorists who are actually Fanon scholars. With the exception of Bhabha's foreword to the London 1986 edition of *Black Skin, White Masks*, and Memmi's review of Caute's and Geismar's texts, none of the other works cited as representative of the theorists under discussion focused on Fanon. Fanon was, in effect, a side issue, which I suppose is consistent with Gates's decentering project and hence may not be of much concern to him. But I don't see how such theorists can then be elevated to the level of standing for the oppressed and the colonized in the effort to determine Fanon's place in colonial discourse and his legitimacy as a voice of the oppressed. Throughout this work, I have used the writings of Renate Zahar, Emmanuel Hansen, L. Adele Jinadu, Hussein Abdilahi Bulhan, all of whom have produced excellent full-length studies on Fanon, and all of whom have a place and a history of praxis among the marginalized. At least in the cases of Zahar, Hansen, and Jinadu, they lived on as well as worked and studied in the African continent. This brings us to some of the theoretical problems with Gates's anti-global theory stand in respect to Fanon.

Gates's project of reading other efforts to analyze Fanon, and from that draw a critical conclusion against any effort to construct a global theory of oppression, is flawed primarily because it presents a straw man. In the first place, implicit in Gates's argument is a criterion that the theorist of colonialism must meet, one that is unrealistic in nature—the interpreters of that theorist or theory must be unequivocal. What are we to make of the hundreds of dissertations, books, and articles on Sartre's philosophical anthropology and his political philosophy? Or Freud's psychoanalysis? Or even Kant's epistemology and his practical philosophy? In effect, Gates is expecting to use the same criterion on human science as that which is used, in very limited cases, in the natural sciences. But his error goes deeper. For the "must meet" proviso that is implicit in his demand *is* a grand demand. It is all-inclusive. Gates has situated himself nicely in the discourse as being immune to the major criterion of that discourse. He has made the classic skeptic's move of placing the burden of validity beyond himself.

Gates writes as though there is nothing to be liberated from but liberation discourse itself. His move reflects the failure of the *rhetoric* of anti-imperialism without an existential component behind that rhetoric. It is as if he were saying, "But for the baggage of race . . . but for the baggage of gender . . . but for the baggage of sexual-orientation . . . but for the baggage of class. . . ." But, as we know, written history now bears tales of US blockades around tiny islands of colored people, rationalizations for atomic bombs in terms of the threat of "irrational"—at times, even "mad"—colored people with nuclear weapons. The correlations between color and poverty, and the uses of colored representatives *against* people of color, are all-too-familiar realities of our contemporary, neocolonial political landscape. In his criticisms of Bhabha, Aijaz Ahmad implicates Gates as well with such accuracy that perhaps our demand for theoretical reflexivity points to a more unified dimension of poststructural analysis than we have previously suggested:

> Edward Said is thus quite astute in describing Ranajit Guha, and by extension the Subalternist project as a whole, as "poststruc-turalist." This same tendency can be witnessed in a great many of the more recent literary theorists themselves, as exemplified by Homi K. Bhabha among others. The positioning of poststructural-ism as the alternative to nationalism is thus quite evident in his own definition of the project as he has assembled it in *Nation and Narration* [which is an intervention into justifications of modernity]. Bhabha, of course, lives in those material conditions of *post*modernity which presume the benefits of modernity as the very ground from which judgements on that past of this *post-* may be delivered. In other words, it takes a very modern, very affluent, very uprooted kind of intellectual to debunk both the

idea of "progress" and the sense of a "long past," not to speak of "modernity" itself, as mere "rationalizations" of "authoritarian tendencies within cultures"—in a theoretical *mélange* which randomly invokes Lévi-Strauss in one phrase, Foucault in another, Lacan in yet another. Those who live within the consequences of that "long past," good and bad, and in places where a majority of the population has been denied access to such benefits of "modernity" as hospitals or better health insurance or even basic literacy, can hardly afford the terms of such thought.[13]

Gates implies that we can simply write away reality, or simply write an alternative one. In spite of literary postmodern claims that writing includes praxis, the focus on words and traditional conceptions of writing suggest that in practice this is a false claim.[14] The degree to which Ahmad's observations parallel Fanon's views is indicative of a reality that may signal the prescience of Robinson's ad hominem attacks on Gates, Bhabha, and Spivak. Just as Fanon became disgusted at the leaders of the negritude movement and found himself disgusted at the individuals he met at the First and Second Congresses of Black Writers and Artists in Paris in 1956 and 1959, so too he might be disgusted at the spectacle that constitutes élite Third World and (exotic) Cultural Studies if he were alive today.[15] It is perhaps a testament to the depth of our conclusion that among these élite theorists, with perhaps the exception of Bhabha, given his dedication to Fanon in his essay, "Interrogating Identity: The Postcolonial Prerogative," the disgust may be mutual. For ultimately, the success of Gates's effort will amount to the preemption of liberation discourse/praxis itself.

The response can be made, however, that the treatment of an anti-liberation discourse as a *reductio ad absurdum* reflects a failure to be radically self-reflexive as well. But our reply is simply that such a move would presuppose a fact/value or description/prescription distinction that obscures a truly radical reading of Fanon's work.[16] Fanon always made sure to criticize value-laden terms, but he didn't criticize them for being value-laden in themselves. His line of criticism was in regard to their being used as a justification *for* value-neutrality. The question of terminology is a matter, then, of the use of certain terms *where relevant*. The relevance question reemerges with determinative force.

We have come, then, to the close of our encounters with Fanon on problems of crisis and the interpretability of human reality. The persistence of the crisis, constructed in terms of European man, has left us with a critical response that ironically manifests itself in both Gates and Robinson. For Gates, a literary theorist, is caught, on the one hand, in the trap of theorizing theory itself by way of centering *literary theory* as a standpoint of validation. Robinson, a political scientist, is caught making the effort to respond to such an assault on theory through the centering of *political theory* as a fundamental point of departure. The question remains of what kind of theory is exemplified, albeit with great fragility, at the point which these two standpoints are even able to recognize Fanon as a subject of inquiry.

We find at least one exemplification of such a "text," if you will, in the recent gathering of scholars from a multitude of disciplines, among whom are included Gates and Robinson, under the title *Reading Rodney King*—a text in which, by the way, references to Fanon are exceeded only by those to Rodney King himself.[17] That these scholars were able to gather around a theme that is fundamentally Fanonian—that is, the beating of a black man by police agents of a racist society and the dynamics of the people's catharsis and the state rationalizations that followed—demonstrates Fanon's existential, historical, and theoretical place among the wretched of the earth *and* those who attempt to study them. Yet, I don't think Fanon would have regarded "reading," albeit intended here as a view of the *academic's* task, to be a suitable response to the beating of Rodney King and the catharsis that followed.[18] This is because for Fanon reading may represent a form of limitation on what one is willing to *do* about the convergence of the racial and the urban in the cities of the United States.

On the matter of text and textuality, then, we find ourselves facing the same kind of questions Husserl faced in his famous lecture, "Philosophy as Rigorous Science": how do we even achieve rigorous theory (which for Husserl is radical) when we are stuck with historians, psychologists, physicists, and (today) literary theorists who practically ontologize their disciplinary perspectives in the name of addressing concerns that may be beyond the scope of their disciplinary assumptions—that is, their disciplinary resources—in advancing radical theories of theory? Husserl concludes:

> It is clear that we cannot wait. We have to take a position, we must bestir ourselves to harmonize the disharmonies in our attitude to reality—to the reality of life, which has significance for us and in which we should have significance—into a rational, even though unscientific, "world-and-life-view." And if the *Weltanschauung* philosopher helps us greatly in this, should we not thank him? No matter how much truth there is in what has just been asserted, no matter how little we should like to miss the exaltation and consolation old and new philosophies offer us, still it must be insisted that we remain aware of the responsibility we have in regard to humanity. For the sake of time we must not sacrifice eternity; in order to alleviate our need, we have no right to bequeath to our posterity need upon need as an eventually ineradicable evil. (p. 141)

Fanon's concerns are in resolute agreement with this dimension of the Husserlian project of radical thinking. We need to go beyond such chauvinism and get on with the business of developing some interesting possibilities.

In identifying European man *qua* European man, we, following Fanon, signal the importance of decentering *him* as designator of human reality. But this does not mean that the project of constructing or engaging in human science must also be abandoned. Instead, in the spirit of Fanon's call for radicality and originality, the challenge becomes one of radical engagement and attuned relevance.

Notes

Preface

1 Dordrecht, the Netherlands: Kluwer Academic Publishers, 1995.

2 See Lewis R. Gordon, *Bad Faith and Antiblack Racism* (Atlantic Highlands, New Jersey: Humanities Press, 1995), chap. 18.

3 Martin J. Matuštík, *Postnational Identity: Critical Theory and Existential Philosophy in Habermas, Kierkegaard, and Havel* (New York: Guilford Press, 1993). Another consequence of those conversations is Matustík's now doing research on Fanon and nationalism, which will be available in his forthcoming book for the State University of New York Press. The book focuses on existential interventions in postmodern and critical theory.

4 Vol. 68, no. 2 (November 1984): 81.

Introduction

1 Emmanuel Hansen, *Frantz Fanon: Social and Political Thought* (Columbus: Ohio State University Press, 1977), 12.

2 (New York: Plenum Press, 1985.)

ONE Fanon as Critique of European Man

1 The full citations for the epigraphs are from Fydor Dostoyevsky, *Great Short Works of Fyodor Dostoyevsky*, trans. David Magarshack and ed. with an intro. by Ronald Hingley (New York: Perennial Classic, Harper &

Row, 1968), 377; W.E.B. Du Bois, *The Souls of Black Folk,* with intros. by Dr. Nathan Hare and Alvin F. Poussaint, M.D. (New York: Signet Classic, 1969), 43–44. Ralph Ellison, *Shadow and Act* (New York: Vintage Books, 1972), 25; and Frantz Fanon, *Black Skin, White Masks,* trans. Charles Lam Markmann (New York: Grove Press, 1967), 109.

2   On Fanon functioning as a voice of the oppressed, especially in terms of the local narratives–grand narrative's debate, see Henry Louis Gates, Jr., "Critical Fanonism," *Critical Inquiry* 17 (1991), 457–478 and Cedric Robinson's critical response to that article, "The Appropriation of Frantz Fanon," *Race & Class* 35, no. 1 (1993),79–91. See also Emmanuel Hansen's *Frantz Fanon,* pp. 9–10, and our discussion in chap. 5.

3   *The Crisis of European Sciences and Transcendental Phenomenology: An Introduction to Phenomenological Philosophy,* trans. with intro. by David Carr (Evanston: Northwestern University Press, 1970), 273.

4   Jürgen Habermas, *Legitimation Crisis,* trans. Thomas McCarthy (Boston: Beacon Press, 1973), passim.

5   I presume the heterosexual black female corollary is a black woman holding a white man's penis.

6   See *The Will to Power,* trans. W. F. Kaufmann and R.J. Hollingdale (New York: Vintage Books, 1968).

7   *The Wretched of the Earth,* preface by Jean-Paul Sartre, trans. Constance Farrington (New York: Grove Press, 1963), 46–47.

8   There are critics. See Albert Memmi's review of Peter Geismar's and David Caute's books on Fanon, "Frozen by Death in the Image of Third World Prophet," *New York Times Book Review* (14 March 1971), 5 and 20; and Gates's "Critical Fanonism," pp. 468–470. For alternative views, see Benita Parry, "Problems in Current Theories of Colonial Discourse," *Oxford Literary Review* 9 (Winter 1987); Cedric Robinson, "The Appropriation of Frantz Fanon"; and Emmanuel Hansen's *Fanon.*

9   *Toward the African Revolution,* trans. Haakon Chevalier (New York: Grove Press, 1967), 53. The quote is from his 1956 resignation letter to the Resident Minister, Governor General of Algeria.

TWO Existential Phenomenology and History

1   The epigraphs are from Merleau-Ponty's "Phenomenology and Sciences of Man," in his *The Primacy of Perception and Other Essays on Phenomenological Psychology, the Philosophy of Art, History and Politics,* ed.

with intro. by James M. Edie (Evanston: Northwestern University Press, 1964), 43–44, also published, with added notes, in Maurice Natanson's, ed., *Phenomenology and the Social Sciences* (Evanston: Northwestern University Press, 1973), 47–48, and Alain Locke's, *The Philosophy of Alain Locke: Harlem Renaissance and Beyond*, Leonard Harris, ed. (Philadelphia: Temple University Press, 1989), 34.

2 *Frantz Fanon* (New York: Viking Press, 1970), 33.

3 This is where the poststructuralists' appropriation of Fanon encounters limitations. Homi Bhabha, for example, attempts to place Lacanian psychoanalysis over Sartre's existential psychoanalysis in blatant disregard of the upshot of the criticism Fanon also raises against Lacan in *Black Skin, White Masks*. (We address Fanon's criticisms of Sartre in this chapter.) In a nutshell, the Lacanian "Where is the phallus?" is a phallic form of questioning already posited from the standpoint of the white man. For discussion of this point, see Lewis R. Gordon, *Bad Faith and Antiblack Racism*, chap. 17. For Homi Bhabha's views, see his "Difference, Discrimination, and the Discourse of Colonialism," in Francis Barker, ed., *The Politics of Theory* (London: Colchester, 1983); "Signs Taken for Wonders: Questions of Ambivalence and Authority Under a Tree Outside Delhi, May 1817," in Henry Louis Gates, Jr., ed., *"Race," Writing, and Difference* (Chicago: University of Chicago Press, 1986); "Remembering Fanon: Self, Psyche and the Colonial Condition," foreword to 1986 London edition of *Black Skin, White Masks* (Pluto Press); and "Interrogating Identity: The Postcolonial Prerogative," in David Theo Goldberg, ed., *Anatomy of Racism* (Minneapolis: University of Minnesota Press, 1990), 183–209.

4 It can be argued, however, that although the transcendental subject is rejected by Sartre, the use of transcendental argumentation and transcendental descriptions remain. See Lewis R. Gordon, "Sartrean Bad Faith and Antiblack Racism," in Steven Crowell, ed., *The Prism of the Self: Essays in Honor of Maurice Natanson* (Dordrecht, the Netherlands: Kluwer Academic Publishers, 1995).

5 It should be noted that this is the "orthodox" view. Although this author is also sympathetic to the unorthodox view, which treats intentions also as intensions, this synopsis holds with either interpretation.

6 For discussion, see Alfred Schutz, *Collected Papers*, Volume 1, *The Problem of Social Reality*, ed. and intro. by Maurice Natanson, with preface by H.L. Van Breda (Hague: Martinus Nijhoff, 1962), 115–116. (Hereafter cited as *The Problem of Social Reality*.)

7 For discussion, see Robert Sokolowski, *Husserlian Meditations: How*

Words Present Things (Evanston: Northwestern University Press, 1974), chap. 1.

8   See Aristotle's *Metaphysics*, trans. W.D. Ross, in *The Basic Works of Aristotle*, ed. with intro. by Richard McKeon (New York: Random House, 1941), Z, 1029b12–1032a10.

9   For discussion, see Edmund Husserl, *Ideas: General Introduction to Pure Phenomenology*, trans. W.R. Boyce Gibson (London: George Allen & Unwin; New York: The Macmillan Company, 1931), First Section, passim, and his *Crisis*, 178. See also Calvin O. Schrag, "Husserl's Legacy in the Postmodern World," *Analecta Husserliana*, Vol. XXX, nos. 127–134 (1991): 127–134. Note, updated translation of *Ideas* is also available under the title, *Ideas Pertaining to a Pure Phenomenology and to a Phenomenological Philosophy*, trans. F. Kersten (Hague: Martinus Nijhoff, 1982).

10 This transcendental move crosses a diverse number of philosophical lines, including pragmatism and linguistic analytical philosophy. For discussion, see Karl Otto Apel, "Is Intentionality More Basic than Linguistic Meaning?" in Ernest Lepore and Robert Van Gulick, eds., *John Searle and His Critics* (Oxford: Blackwell Publishers, 1991), 31–56.

11 For a discussion and critique of Husserl's claim to radicality in this dimension of his thought, see Calvin O. Schrag's *Radical Reflection and the Origin of the Human Sciences* (West Lafayette, Indiana: Purdue University Press, 1980), 16–24.

12 See R. Philip Buckley, "A Critique of Husserl's Notion of Crisis," in Arleen B. Dallery, Charles E. Schott, and Holley Roberts, eds., *Crises in Continental Philosophy* (Albany: State University of New York Press, 1990), 23–33, where it is pointed out that Husserl's is a philosophy of crisis straight through from the early works to the *Crisis*.

13 As we shall see, this is the meaning behind Fanon's introductory remark in *Black Skin, White Masks*, that man is also a *yes*.

14 See Merleau-Ponty's *Phenomenology of Perception*, trans. Colin Smith (Atlantic Highlands, New Jersey: Humanities Press, 1961); and *The Visible and the Invisible*, trans. Alphonso Lingis, and Claude Lefort, ed. (Evanston: Northwestern University Press, 1968).

15 See Alfred Schutz's *Phenomenology of the Social World*, trans. George Walsh and Frederick Lehnert, with intro. by George Walsh (Evanston: Northwestern University Press, 1967); and *The Problem of Social Reality*. See also Maurice Natanson, *Anonymity: A Study in the Philosophy of Alfred Schutz* (Bloomington: Indiana University Press, 1986).

16 For more discussion, see chap. 3.

Notes

17   From Husserl, *Phenomenology and the Crisis of Philosophy: "Philosophy as Rigorous Science" and "Philosophy and the Crisis of European Man,"* trans. with an intro. by Quentin Lauer (New York: Harper Torchbooks, 1965), 147. Originally published as "Philosophie als strenge Wissenschaft," *Logos,* I (1910–1911), 289–341.

18   Elizabeth A. Behnke, "On Phenomenology and Medicine," *Study Project in Phenomenology of the Body Newsletter* 6, no. 2 (Fall 1993), 10.

19   For more discussion, see Lewis R. Gordon, *Bad Faith and Antiblack Racism,* especially Part I.

20   For succinct discussion, see *Search for a Method,* trans. with an intro. by Hazel Barnes (New York: Vintage Books, 1968), chap. 3.

21   Volume 1, *Theory of Practical Ensembles,* trans. Alan Sheridan-Smith, Jonathan Rée, ed. (London and New York: Verso, 1991).

22   For the classic statement on this view, see Karl Marx, "On the Jewish Question," in Robert C. Tucker, ed., *The Marx-Engels Reader,* Second Edition (New York: W.W. Norton & Company, 1978), 26–52.

23   For similar discussion, see Maurice Natanson, *Husserl: Philosopher of Infinite Tasks* (Evanston: Northwestern University Press, 1973), chap. 9.

24   For more discussion of the convergence of Marxism and the philosophy of existence, see chap. 3 below; and Sartre's *Search for a Method,* and Jameson's *Marxism and Form: Twentieth-Century Dialectical Theories of Literature* (Princeton: Princeton University Press, 1971), chap. 4; and also my discussion in chap. 26 of *Bad Faith and Antiblack Racism.*

25   See *Bad Faith and Antiblack Racism,* passim. For short discussions, see the author's "Racism as a Form of Bad Faith," *American Philosophical Association Newsletter on Philosophy and the Black Experience* 92, no. 2 (1993), 6–8; and "Sartrean Bad Faith and Antiblack Racism," in Steven Crowell, ed., *The Prism of the Self.* See also Tommy Lott, "Du Bois on Invention of Race," *The Philosophical Forum* XXIV, nos. 1–3 (Fall–Spring 1992–93): 166–187.

26   See also Simone de Beauvoir, *The Force of Circumstances,* trans. Richard Howard (New York: Putnam, 1965), 592, for an account of Sartre's meeting with Fanon in Rome, where Fanon argued that Sartre is ultimately "guilty" of being French.

27   For discussion, see C.W. Cassinelli's *Total Revolution: A Comparative Study of Germany under Hitler, the Soviet Union under Stalin, and China under Mao* (Santa Barbara: Clio Books, 1976), Part II.

28   For discussion, see *The Philosophy of Alain Locke,* 112–113.

29 See chap. 4 below, where we point out the tragic dimensions of this question.

30 For more discussion, see *Bad Faith and Antiblack Racism*, chaps. 12–14.

31 For the significance of the relationship between the colloquial or everyday sense of having a history and this understanding of bad faith, see Maurice Natanson's *The Journeying Self: A Study in Philosophy and Social Role* (Reading, Massachusetts: Addison-Wesley Publishing Company, 1970), 91. One's history is an aspect of one's facticity. To deny it is a form of bad faith. See also our discussions of the everyday in chap. 3

32 See G.W. F. Hegel's *The Philosophy of History*, trans. with a preface by J. Sebree, a preface by Charles Hegel, and a new intro. by C. J. Friedrich (New York: Dover Publications, 1956), 107, and Part III; as well as his *Philosophy of Right*, trans. with notes by T.M. Knox (London: Oxford University Press, 1967), especially 51. See also Charles Taylor, *Hegel and Modern Society* (New York: Cambridge University Press, 1979), 100–101.

33 Frederick Douglass, *Narrative of the Life of Frederick Douglass, An American Slave, Written by Himself* (New York: New American Library, 1968), 81–82.

34 For discussion of negritude, see Renate Zahar's *Frantz Fanon: Colonialism and Alienation, Concerning Frantz Fanon's Political Theory*, trans. Willfried F. Feuser (New York: Monthly Review Press, 1974).

35 "Black Orpheus," trans. John MacCombie, in *"What is Literature?" and Other Essays*, ed. with intro. by Steven Ungar (Cambridge, Mass.: Harvard University Press, 1988), 326–330.

36 For a discussion of Sartre's conception of progress, see Ronald Aronson, "Sartre on Progress," in Christina Howells, ed., *The Cambridge Companion to Sartre* (Cambridge, England: Cambridge University Press, 1992), 261–292. Aronson's discussion is heavily influenced by the second (unfinished) volume of Sartre's *Critique*, edited by Arlette Elkaïm-Sartre, *The Intelligibility of History*, trans. Quintin Hoare (London: Verso, 1991). See also Fredric Jameson, *Marxism and Form*, chap. 4.

37 For a developed, phenomenological discussion of place and alienation, see Edward Casey, *Getting Back into Place: Toward a Renewed Understanding of the Place-World* (Bloomington: Indiana University Press, 1993), especially 307–310 and 313.

38 For discussion, our chap. 3.

39 This is not the place for a discussion of the meaning and social-scien-

Notes

tific and phenomenological validity of "class." The literature on the concept is vast, and here I only hint at some of Sartre's interpretations. But Sartre's most sustained analysis of the concept can be found in his *Critique.* For commentary, see William L. McBride, *Sartre's Political Theory* (Bloomington: Indiana University Press, 1991), especially 78–79 and 164–166. See also Jameson's *Marxism and Form,* 215–19 and 297.

40 *A Dying Colonialism,* trans. Haakon Chevalier with an introduction by Adolfo Gilly (New York: Grove Weidenfield, 1965), 44.

41 We have already mentioned Homi Bhabha's efforts to interpret Fanon in a postmodern (poststructural or deconstructive) way. Although Fanon would agree that there is a postcolonial prerogative, I suggest that he would also add that asserting our contemporary neocolonial historical situation as a postcolonial one is a form of bad faith. Postcolonial discourse in colonial and neocolonial times serves, ultimately, as sustenance for the *status quo.* Fanon was aware that colonial categories of identity needed to be criticized with circumspection and a critical historical outlook—ultimately, critical good faith—for a revolutionary praxis to emerge. For more discussion, see chap. 5 below.

42 For a similar view, see L. Adele Jinadu's *Fanon: In Search of the African Revolution* (London: KPI/Routledge & Kegan Paul, 1986). We will examine these themes in our chaps. 3–5 below.

THREE Racism, Colonialism, and Anonymity

1 The epigraphs are from *The Philosophy of Alain Locke* (34–38), *Radical Reflections* (62), and *The Phenomenology of Perception* (85).

2 We have cited Schutz's relevant work. See also Natanson's *Anonymity* for an explication of these phenomena.

3 For discussion of these kinds of observations during slavery, see Herbert G. Gutman, *The Black Family in Slavery and Freedom 1750–1925* (New York: Vintage, 1976).

4 For full treatment of this view, see Lewis R. Gordon, ed., *Existence in Black: An Anthology of Black Existential Philosophy* (New York and London: Routledge, 1996).

5 Hountondji's *African Philosophy: Myth and Reality,* trans. Henri Evans, with the collaboration of Jonathan Rée (London: Hutchinson University Library for Africa, 1983) is arguably a work in phenomenology of culture, in spite of his Marxist commitments (which this author regards as not being contradictory with phenomenology).

111

6   Max Weber, *The Theory of Social and Economic Organization*, trans. A.M. Henderson and Talcott Parsons, with an intro. by Talcott Parsons, ed. (New York: The Free Press, 1966), 88. This unfinished work is the most detailed treatment of his conception of social science. It was originally published in 1922, in Tübingen, under the title *Wirtschaft und Gesellschaft*.

7   Alfred Schutz, *Collected Papers*, Volume II: *Studies in Social Theory*, ed. with intro. by Arvid Brodersen (Hague: Martinus Nijhoff, 1964), 24. Hereafter cited as *Studies in Social Theory*.

8   See Schutz's *The Problem of Social Reality*, 59; and Natanson's *Anonymity*, 9–10.

9   See *Translations from the Philosophical Writings of Gottlob Frege*, Second Revised Edition, trans. Peter Geach and Max Black, eds. (Oxford and New York: Oxford University Press, 1960), and Michael Dummett, *Frege: Philosophy of Language*, Second Edition (Cambridge, Mass: Harvard University Press, 1981), especially chap. 5.

10 For discussion, see David Theo Goldberg, *Racist Culture: Philosophy and the Politics of Meaning* (Oxford: Blackwell, 1993), chaps. 3, 4, and 6.

11 See, for example, Mill's *A System of Logic* (London: Longman's, 1843); Popper's *The Poverty of Historicism* (New York: Harper Torchbooks, Harper & Row, 1964); and Quine's *Ontological Relativity and Other Essays* (New York: Columbia University Press, 1969).

12 John Searle, "Response: Meaning, Intentionality, and Speech Acts," in *John Searle and His Critics*, 82.

13 This is a thorny issue in the history of philosophy. See Aristotle's *Metaphysics*, M (XIII), 1076a9–1078b5, 180a15–180b35; Gottlob Frege, *Foundations of Arithmetic: A Logico-mathematical Enquiry into the Concept of Number*, trans. J.L. Austin (Oxford: Oxford University Press, 1950); Bertrand Russell's *Introduction to Mathematical Philosophy* (New York: Simon & Schuster, 1919), chapters 6 and 7; and *The Problems of Philosophy* (London: Oxford University Press, 1912), 77; Husserl, *Formal and Transcendental Logic*, trans. Dorion Cairns (Hague: Martinus Nijhoff, 1969); Robert Sokolowski, *Husserlian Meditations* (Evanston: Northwestern University Press, 1974), 100; Charles Parsons, "Foundations of Mathematics," in Paul Edwards, ed., *The Encyclopedia of Philosophy*, Vol. 5 (New York: Macmillan & Free Press, 1967), 188–213; and Stephen Barker, "Number," ibid, 526–530.

14 See Merleau-Ponty's discussion of induction in his essay, "Phenomenology and the Sciences of Man" and Natanson's discussion of the suppression of primes in the third chapter of *Anonymity*.

15 Max Weber, *From Max Weber: Essays in Sociology*, trans. with intro. by

Notes

H.H. Gerth and C. Wright Mills, eds. (New York: Oxford University Press, 1946), 323–324. Weber's most detailed treatment of these matters can be found in *The Theory of Social and Economic Organization*.

16 For discussion of this error, see Merleau-Ponty's criticisms of John Stuart Mill in *The Primacy of Perception*, 69–70; same essay, "Phenomenology and the Sciences of Man," included in Natanson, ed., *Phenomenology and the Social Sciences*, 77–78.

17 For succinct discussion of phenomenological essence, see Merleau-Ponty's *Phenomenology of Perception*, xiv–xvii and Schutz's *The Problem of Social Reality*, 113–15.

18 We have already identified the poststructuralist and literary postmodernist standpoints. For other recent examples, see Michael Walzer, *The Company of Critics: Social Criticism and Political Commitment in the Twentieth Century* (New York: Basic Books, 1988), 150–51; and Cornel West, *Keeping Faith: Philosophy and Race in America* (New York and London: Routledge, 1993), 13. Representative (and more substantial) early versions of these criticisms can be found in Horace B. Davis *Toward a Marxist Theory of Nationalism* (New York: Monthly Review Press, 1978), chap. 8; and Jack Woddis, *New Theories of Revolution: A Commentary on the Views of Frantz Fanon, Régis Debray and Herbert Marcuse* (New York: International Publishers, 1972), chap. 2.

19 Although on page 88 of *Black Skin, White Masks* Fanon speaks disparagingly of Mannoni's efforts at phenomenology and psycho-analysis, it should be borne in mind that he never once rejects Sartre's nor Merleau-Ponty's phenomenological methodologies. In fact, he takes phenomenology in rather original directions of his own, as we have pointed out in our discussion of anonymity and embodiment. For a work that concurs with our view, see Bulhan's *Frantz Fanon and the Psychology of Oppression*. Bulhan describes the chapter, "The Fact of Blackness," in *Black Sin, White Masks*, as "a phenomenological description of a psycho-existential crisis" in addition to Fanon's negotiating his way through negritude. For a nonphenomenological defense of Fanon, see also Jinadu's *Fanon: In Search of the African Revolution*.

20 Fanon maintains this position throughout his thought. See our fourth chapter below.

21 For Freire's view, see *Pedagogy of the Oppressed*, trans. Myra Bergman Ramos (New York: Continuum, 1990).

22 Eva Figes, *Tragedy and Social Evolution* (New York: Persea Books, 1976), 36.

FOUR Tragic Violence and Philosophical Anthropology

1   The epigraphs are from Aristotle's *Poetics*, in Richard McKeon, ed., *The Basic Works of Aristotle* (1448a), and Figes's *Tragedy and Social Evolution* (33), and Douglass's *Narrative* (83).

2   Hannah Arendt, *On Violence* (New York: Harcourt Brace Jovanovich, 1970), 14, n. 19. For discussion of the flaws in Arendt's criticisms of Fanon, see Jinadu's *Fanon*, 92, 93, and 231; and Bulhan's *Fanon and the Psychology of Oppression*, 145–148.

3   This is my revision of Ingram Bywater's trans. of the *Poetics* in Richard McKeon, ed. *The Basic Works of Aristotle*. The Greek version from which my revisions were determined is *Aristotle "The Poetics"; Longinus "On the Sublime"; Demetrius "On Style,"* with an accompanying English trans. by W. Hamilton Fyfe (London: William Heinemann, 1932).

4   For discussion, see Hansen's *Frantz Fanon*, chap. 5, and Jinadu's *Fanon*, chap. 4.

5   For his sustained discussions on society with the use of characters in myths and classic tragedies, see Freud's *Civilization and Its Discontents*, Standard Edition, trans. James Strachey (New York: W.W. Norton & Company, 1961), and *Character and Culture*, Philip Rieff, ed. (New York: Collier Books, 1963). See also his *An Outline of Psycho-Analysis*, Revised Edition, trans. James Strachey (New York: W.W. Norton & Company, 1969).

6   For Hegel's discussion of tragedy, see his *Philosophy of Fine Art*, trans. F.P.B. Somaston, 4 vols. (London: G. Bell and Sons, 1920); as well as *The Introduction to Hegel's Philosophy of Fine Art*, trans. Bernard Bosanquet (London: K. Paul, Trench & Co., 1886).

7   *The World as Will and Idea*, Vol. I, Seventh Edition, trans. R.B. Haldane and J. Kemp (London: Kegan Paul, Trench, Trubner & Co., 1883), 326. The seventh edition of all three volumes were published in 1883 by Kegan Paul, Trench, Trubner & Co.

8   *The Birth of Tragedy*, trans. Francis Golffing (Garden City, New York: Doubleday and Company, 1956), especially 46–69.

9   For developed discussion on crowds, see Elias Canetti, *Crowds and Power*, trans. Carol Stewart (New York: Farrar Straus Giroux, 1984).

10 For the entire story, see David Grene and Richmond Lattimore, eds., *Sophocles I: "Oedipus the King," Translated by David Grene, "Oedipus at Colonus," Translated by Robert Fitzgerald, and "Antigone," Translated by Elizabeth Wyckoff* (Chicago: University of Chicago Press, 1954).

Notes

11 Blacks hold a special place in the people-of-color designation because of the mythology that emerged around blackness and sin, wherein black people have been historically synonymous with "cursed" people. For discussion, see Eulalio Baltazar's *The Dark Center: A Process Theology of Blackness* (New York: Paulist Press, 1973), and *Bad Faith and Antiblack Racism*, Parts III and IV.

12 This is the core of the crisis dimension of our discussions in chaps. 1 and 2 above.

13 William R. Jones, "Liberation Strategies in Black Theology: Mao, Martin, or Malcolm?," in Leonard Harris, ed., *Philosophy Born of Struggle: Anthology of Afro-American Philosophy from 1917* (Dubuque, Iowa: Kendall/Hunt Publishing Company, 1983), 238.

14 For a summary of Fanon's usage and citation of the literature on violence, see especially Hansen's *Frantz Fanon*, 116–121, and 168; and Jinadu's *Fanon*, 14, and 44–52.

15 See also Robinson's *Black Marxism: The Making of the Black Radical Tradition* (London: Zed Press, 1983), especially 243

16 *The Black Jacobins: Toussaint L'Ouverture and the San Domingo Revolution*, Second Edition, revised (New York: Vintage Books, 1989), 88–89.

FIVE Fanon's Continued Relevance

1 The epigraph is from *Sappho: The Poems*, Revised Edition, trans. Sasha Newborn (Santa Barbara: Bandanna Books, 1993), 11.

2 For Jean-François Lyotard's notion of grand theory, see his *The Postmodern Condition: A Report on Knowledge*, trans. Geoff Bennington and Brian Massumi (Minneapolis: University of Minnesota Press, 1984). And for recent discussion and critique, see Calvin O. Schrag, *The Resources of Rationality: A Response to the Postmodern Challenge* (Bloomington: Indiana University Press, 1992).

3 The Said article is from *Critical Inquiry* 15 (Winter 1989), and the passage quoted is from page 223.

4 For discussion of Fanon's sense of humor, see Bulhan's discussion of his childhood and personality, *Frantz Fanon and the Psychology of Oppression*, chap. 2.

5 See also Marx's *The German Ideology*, in Robert Tucker, ed., *The Marx-Engels Reader*, 149.

6 C.L.R. James, "Black Power," in Anna Grimshaw, ed., *The C.L.R. James Reader* (Oxford: Blackwell, 1993), 367.

7 See especially Robinson's "The Appropriation of Frantz Fanon," 82.

8   See Jack Woddis' *New Theories of Revolution* and Horace Davis's *Toward a Marxist Theory of Nationalism* for representative critics of Fanon in this regard.

9   See Fanon's discussion of Hegel in *Black Skin, White Masks*, 216–22.

10   For discussion of Fanon's family lineage, see Richard C. Onwuanibe, Richard C. *A Critique of Revolutionary Humanism: Frantz Fanon* (St. Louis, Missouri: Warren H. Green, 1983), vii–viii.

11   For more discussion, see also Renate Zahar, *L'Oeuvre de Frantz Fanon* (Paris: Maspéro, 1979), especially 7.

12   See also Lou Turner and John Alan, *Frantz Fanon, Soweto and American Black Thought*, New and Expanded Edition (Chicago: News and Letters, 1986), 50.

13   Aijaz Ahmad, *In Theory: Classes, Nations, Literatures* (London: Verso, 1992), 68–69.

14   For a critical discussion of this type of "writing," see Lewis R. Gordon, *Her Majesty's Other Children: Philosophical Sketches from a Neocolonial Age* (Atlantic Highlands: Humanities Press, 1996).

15   We have been discussing Fanon's criticism of focusing on culture alone as a standpoint of critique. For more discussion, see Lou Turner and John Alan, *Frantz Fanon, Soweto, and American Black Thought*, especially 50, and René Depestre's essay, "Critique of Negritude," in the appendices of the same volume, 70–73.

16   For discussion of this matter, see J. Adele Jinadu's *Fanon*, chap. 4.

17   Robert Gooding-Williams, ed., *Reading Rodney King: Reading Urban Uprising* (New York and London: Routledge, 1993). Fanon has been cited in so many works since 1990 that an independent volume of Fanon citations would emerge if they were all documented.

18   Although *Reading Rodney King* avoids this pitfall, there have been studies of black folk that stand as egregious examples of textual reductionism, in some cases, to the point of being clear examples of racism. For a volume of essays on problems of treating human beings as texts, see Lewis R. Gordon and Renée T. White, eds., *Black Texts and Black Textuality: Constructing and De-Constructing Blackness* (forthcoming).

Bibliography

Adams, Paul. "The Social Psychiatry of Frantz Fanon." *American Journal of Psychiatry* 127 (December 1970): 109–114.

Ahmad, Aijaz. 1992. *In Theory: Classes, Nations, Literatures*. London: Verso.

Anton, Antole. "Letter to the Editor." *Proceedings and Addresses of the American Philosophical Association* 68, no. 2 (November 1994): 80–82.

Apel, Karl Otto. "Is Intentionality More Basic than Linguistic Meaning?" In *John Searle and His Critics*. Oxford: Blackwell, 1991: 31–56. (See Searle.)

Arendt, Hannah. 1969. *On Violence*. New York: Harcourt Brace & Javanovitch.

Aristotle. 1932. In *Aristotle: "The Poetics"; Longinus "On the Sublime"; Demetrius "On Style."* W. Hamilton Fyfe, ed. and trans., London: William Heinemann: 4–118.

———. 1941. *The Basic Works of Aristotle*. Ed. with an intro. by Richard McKeon. New York: Random House.

Aronson, Ronald. 1992. "Sartre on Progress." In *The Cambridge Companion to Sartre*, ed. by Christina Howells. Cambridge, England: Cambridge University Press.

Baltazar, Eulalio. 1973. *The Dark Center: A Process Theology of Blackness*. New York: Paulist Press.

Bibliography

Beauvoir, Simone de. 1965. *The Force of Circumstances.* Trans. by Richard Howard. New York: G.P. Putnam's Sons.

Beck, Elizabeth A. "On Phenomenology and Medicine." *Study Project in Phenomenology of the Body Newsletter* 6, no. 2 (Fall 1993): 9–10.

Berger, Roger. "Contemporary Anglophone Literary Theory: The Return of Fanon." *Research in African Literature* (1990).

Bhabha, Homi. 1983. "Difference, Discrimination, and the Discourse of Colonialism." In *The Politics of Theory,* ed. by Francis Barker. London: Colchester.

————. 1986. "Signs Taken for Wonders: Questions of Ambivalence and Authority Under a Tree Outside Delhi, May 1817." In *"Race," Writing, and Difference.* Chicago: University of Chicago Press, 1986. (See Gates).

————. 1986. "Remembering Fanon: Self, Psyche and the Colonial Condition." Foreword to London, 1986 edition of *Black Skin, White Masks.* Pluto Press.

————. 1990. "Interrogating Identity: The Postcolonial Prerogative." In *Anatomy of Racism.* Minneapolis: University of Minnesota Press, 1990: 183–209. (See Goldberg).

Blackey, Robert. "Fanon and Cabral: A Contrast in Theories of Revolution for Africa." *Journal of Modern African Studies* 12 (June 1974): 191–209.

Buckley, R. Philip. 1990. "A Critique of Husserl's Notion of Crisis." In *Crises in Continental Philosophy.* Ed. by Arleen B. Dallery, Charles E. Schott, and Holley Roberts. Albany: State University of New York Press.

Bulhan, Hussein Abdilahi. 1985. *Frantz Fanon and the Psychology of Oppression.* New York: Plenum Press.

Cabral, Amilcar. 1969. *Revolution in Guinea: Selected Texts.* Ed. and trans. by Richard Handyside. New York: Monthly Review Press.

————. 1970. *National Liberation and Culture.* Occasional Paper no. 57. Syracuse: Maxwell Graduate School, Syracuse University.

Camus, Albert. 1956. *The Rebel: An Essay on Man in Revolt.* Trans. by Anthony Bower, with a foreword by Sir Herbert Read. New York: Vintage Books.

————. 1960. *Resistance, Rebellion, and Death.* Trans. with an Introduction by Justin O'Brien. New York: Vintage Books.

Bibliography

Canetti, Elias. 1984. *Crowds and Power.* Trans. by Carol Stewart. New York: Farrar Straus Giroux.

Carmichael, Stokeley, and Charles Hamilton. 1967. *Black Power.* New York: Vintage.

Casey, Edward. 1993. *Getting Back into Place: Toward a Renewed Understanding of the Place-World.* Bloomington: Indiana University Press.

Cassinelli, C.W. 1976. *Total Revolution: A Comparative Study of Germany under Hitler, the Soviet Union under Stalin, and China under Mao.* Santa Barbara: Clio Books.

Caute, David. 1970. *Frantz Fanon.* New York: Viking Press.

Césaire, Aimé. 1972. *Discourse on Colonialism.* New York: Monthly Review Press.

Cherif, Mohamed. "Frantz Fanon: la Science au service de la révolution." *Jeune Afrique,* no. 295, (4 September 1966): 24.

Cruse, Harold. 1967. *The Crisis of the Negro Intellectual.* New York: Quill.

Davis, Horace. 1978. *Toward a Marxist Theory of Nationalism.* New York: Monthly Review Press.

Debray, Régis. 1967. *Revolution in the Revolution?* New York: Grove Press.

Depestre, René. 1986. "Critique of Negritude." In *Frantz Fanon, Soweto, and American Black Thought.* Chicago: News and Letters, 1986: 70–73. (See Turner and Alan.)

Dostoyevsky, Fyodor. 1968. *Great Short Works of Fyodor Dostoyevsky.* Ed. with an intro. by Ronald Hingley. New York: Perennial Classic, Harper & Row.

Douglass, Frederick. 1968. *Narrative of the Life of Frederick Douglass, An American Slave, Written by Himself.* New York: New American Library.

DuBois, W.E.B. 1968. *The Autobiography of W.E.B. DuBois: A Soliloquy on Viewing My Life from the Last Decade of Its First Century.* Ed. by Herbert Aptheker. New York: International Publishers.

———. 1969. *The Souls of Black Folk.* Intro. by Dr. Nathan Hare and Alvin F. Poussaint, M.D. New York: Signet Classic.

Ellison, Ralph. 1953. *Invisible Man.* New York: New American Library.

———. 1972. *Shadow and Act.* New York: Vintage Books.

Fanon, Frantz. 1952. *Peau Noire, Masques Blancs.* Paris: Editions de Seuil.

———. 1961. *Les Damnés de la Terre.* François Maspero.

119

Bibliography

————. 1963. *The Wretched of the Earth.* Trans. by Constance Farrington. New York: Grove Press.

————. 1965. *A Dying Colonialism.* Trans. by Haakon Chevalier with an introduction by Adolfo Gilly. New York: Grove Weidenfield.

————. 1967. *Black Skin, White Masks.* Trans. by Charles Lam Markmann. New York: Grove Press.

————. 1967. *Toward the African Revolution.* Trans. by Haakon Chevalier. New York: Grove Press.

————. 1968. *Sociologie d'une Révolution.* Paris: François Maspero.

————. 1979. *Pour la Révolution Africaine: Écrits Politiques.* Paris: François Maspero.

Figes, Eva. 1976. *Tragedy and Social Evolution.* New York: Persea Books.

Frege, Gottlob. 1950. *Foundations of Arithmetic: A Logico-mathematical Enquiry into the Concept of Number.* Trans. by J.L. Austin. Oxford: Oxford University Press.

————. 1960. *Translations from the Philosophical Writings of Gottlob Frege,* 2nd revised edition. Ed. and trans. by Peter Geach and Max Black. Oxford and New York: Oxford University Press.

Freire, Paulo. 1990. *Pedagogy of the Oppressed.* Trans. by Myra Bergman Ramos. New York: Continuum.

Freud, Sigmund. 1961. *Civilization and Its Discontents.* Standard Edition. Trans. by James Strachey. New York: W.W. Norton & Company.

————. 1963. *Character and Culture.* Ed. by Philip Rieff. New York: Collier Books.

————. 1969. *An Outline of Psycho-Analysis.* Revised Edition. Trans. by James Strachey. New York: W.W. Norton & Company.

Gates, Jr., Henry Louis. 1991. "Critical Fanonism." *Critical Inquiry* 17: 457–478.

————. Ed. 1986. *"Race," Writing and Difference.* Chicago: University of Chicago Press.

Geismar, Peter. 1971. *Frantz Fanon.* New York: Dial Press.

————. "A Biographical Sketch." *Monthly Review* 21 (May 1969): 22–30.

Gendzier, Irene. 1973. *Frantz Fanon: A Critical Study.* New York: Pantheon Books.

Bibliography

Gooding-Williams, Robert, ed. 1993. *Reading Rodney King, Reading Urban Uprising.* New York and London: Routledge.

Goldberg, David Theo. 1993. *Racist Culture: Philosophy and the Politics of Meaning.* Oxford: Blackwell.

———. Ed. 1990. *Anatomy of Racism.* Minneapolis and London: University of Minnesota Press.

Gordon, Lewis R. 1993. "Racism as a Form of Bad Faith." *American Philosophical Association Newsletter on Philosophy and the Black Experience,* 92, no. 2: 6–8.

———. 1995. *Bad Faith and Antiblack Racism.* Atlantic Highlands, New Jersey: Humanities Press.

———. 1995a. "Sartrean Bad Faith and Antiblack Racism." In *The Prism of the Self: Essays in Honor of Maurice Natanson,* ed. Steven Crowell. Dordrecht, the Netherlands: Kluwer Academic Publishers.

———. 1996. *Her Majesty's Other Children: Philosophical Sketches from a Neocolonial Age.* Atlantic Highlands, New Jersey: The Humanities Press.

———. 1996a. *Existence in Black: An Anthology of Black Existential Philosophies.* New York and London: Routledge.

Gordon, Lewis R. and Reneé T. White, eds. Forthcoming. *Black Texts and Black Textuality: Constructing and De-Constructing Blackness.*

Gutman, Herbert G. 1976. *The Black Family in Slavery and Freedom 1750–1925.* New York: Vintage.

Habermas, Jürgen. 1973. *Legitimation Crisis.* Trans. by Thomas McCarthy. Boston: Beacon Press.

Hansen, Emmanuel. "Frantz Fanon: A Bibliographical Essay." *Pan-African Journal* 5 (Winter 1972): 387–405.

———. "Frantz Fanon: Portrait of a Revolutionary Intellectual." *Transition,* no. 46 (October–December 1974): 25–36.

———. 1977. *Frantz Fanon: Social and Political Thought.* Columbus: Ohio State University Press.

Hegel, G. W. F. 1886. *The Introduction to Hegel's Philosophy of Fine Art.* Trans. by Bernard Bosanquet. London: K. Paul, Trench & Co.

———. 1920. *The Philosophy of Fine Art.* Volumes I–IV. Trans. by F.P.B. Somaston. London: G. Bell and Sons.

———. 1956. *The Philosophy of History.* Trans. with a pref. by J. Sebree, a pref. by Charles Hegel, and a new introd. by C.J. Friedrich. NY: Dover Publications.

———. 1967. *The Philosophy of Right.* Trans. with notes by T.M. Knox. London: Oxford University Press.

———. 1977. *Phenomenology of Spirit.* Trans. by A.V. Miller, with analysis of the text and foreword by J.N. Findlay. Oxford: Oxford University Press.

Husserl, Edmund. 1910–1911. "Philosophie als strenge Wissenschaft." *Logos* I : 289–341.

———. 1931. *Ideas: General Introduction to Pure Phenomenology.* Trans. by W.R. Boyce Gibson. London: George Allen & Unwin; New York: Macmillan.

———. 1960. *Cartesian Meditations: An Introduction to Phenomenology.* Trans. by Dorion Cairns. Dordrecht: Martinus Nijhoff.

———. 1965. *Phenomenology and the Crisis of Philosophy: "Philosophy as a Rigorous Science" and "Philosophy and the Crisis of European Man."* Trans. with an intro. by Quentin Lauer. New York: Harper Torchbooks.

———. 1969. *Formal and Transcendental Logic.* Trans. by Dorion Cairns. Hague: Martinus Nijhoff.

———. 1970. *The Crisis of European Sciences and Transcendental Phenomenology: An Introduction to Phenomenological Philosophy.* Trans. with an intro. by David Carr. Evanston: Northwestern University Press.

———. 1982. *Ideas Pertaining to a Pure Phenomenology and to a Phenomenological Philosophy.* Trans. by F. Kersten. Hague: Martinus Nijhoff.

Irele, Abiola. "Literature and Ideology in Martinique: Reé Maran, Aimé Césaire, Frantz Fanon." *Research Review* 5, no. 3 (1969): 1–32.

James, C.L.R. 1989. *The Black Jacobins: Toussaint L'Ouverture and the San Domingo Revolution.* Second Revised Edition. New York: Vintage.

———. 1993. *The C.L.R. James Reader.* Ed. with intro. by Anna Grimshaw. Oxford: Blackwell Publishers.

Jameson, Fredric. 1971. *Marxism and Form: Twentieth-Century Dialectical Theories of Literature.* Princeton: Princeton University Press.

Bibliography

Jinadu, L. Adele. 1986. *Fanon: In Search of the African Revolution.* London: KPI/Routledge & Kegan Paul.

Jones, William R. 1983. "Liberation Strategies in Black Theology: Mao, Martin, or Malcolm?" In Leonard Harris, editor. *Philosophy Born of Struggle: Anthology of Afro-American Philosophy from 1917,* ed. by Leonard Harris. Dubuque, Iowa: Kendall/Hunt.

Koundoura, Maria. "Naming Gayatyri Spivak." *Stanford Humanities Review* (1989).

Leder, Drew. 1990. *The Absent Body.* Chicago: University of Chicago Press.

Lenin, V.I. 1969. *What Is To Be Done?: Burning Questions of Our Movement.* Trans. Joe Fineberg and George Hannah. New York: International Publishers.

Locke, Alain. 1989. *The Philosophy of Alain Locke: Harlem Renaissance and Beyond,* ed. by Leonard Harris. Philadelphia: Temple University Press.

Lott, Tommy L. "Du Bois on the Invention of Race." *The Philosophical Forum.* XXIV, nos. 1–3 (Fall–Spring 1992–93): 166–87.

Lowenthal, David. "Race and Color in the West Indies." *Daedalus* 96, no. 2 (Spring 1967): 580–626.

Lyotard, Jean-François. 1984. *The Postmodern Condition: A Report on Knowledge.* Trans. by Geoff Bennington and Brian Massumi. Minneapolis: University of Minnesota Press.

Martin, Guy. "Fanon's Relevance to Contemporary African Political Thought." *Ufahamu* 4 (Winter 1974): 11–34.

Martin, Tony. "Rescuing Fanon from the Critics." *African Studies Review* 13 (December 1970): 381–399.

Matustík, Martin. 1993. *Postnational Identity: Critical Theory and Existential Philosophy in Habermas, Kierkegaard, and Havel.* New York and London: Guilford Press.

McBride, William L. 1991. *Sartre's Political Theory.* Bloomington: Indiana University Press.

McCulloch, Jock. 1983. *Black Soul, White Artifact: Fanon's Clinical Psychology and Social Theory.* London: Cambridge University Press.

Memmi, Albert. 1968. *Dominated Man.* New York: Orion Press.

———. 1971. "Frozen by Death in the Image of Third World Prophet." *New York Times Book Review* (14 May 1971): 5, 20.

————. 1971. "La Vie impossible de Frantz Fanon." *Esprit* (September 1971): 248–273.

Merleau-Ponty, Maurice. 1961. *Phenomenology of Perception.* Trans. by Colin Smith. Atlantic Highlands, New Jersey: Humanities Press.

————. 1964. *"The Primacy of Perception" and Other Essays on Phenomenological Psychology, the Philosophy of Art, History and Politics.* Ed. with an intro. by James M. Edie. Evanston: Northwestern University Press.

————. 1968. *The Visible and the Invisible: Followed by Working Notes.* Ed. by Claude Lefort and trans. by Alphonso Lingis. Evanston: Northwestern University Press.

Mill, John Stuart. 1843. *A System of Logic.* London: Longman's.

Natanson, Maurice. 1962. *Edmund Husserl: Philosopher of Infinite Tasks.* Hague: Martinus Nijhoff.

————. Ed. 1963. *Phenomenology and Social Reality: Essays in Memory of Alfred Schutz.* New York: Random House.

————. 1970. *The Journeying Self: A Study in Philosophy and Social Role.* Reading, Mass.: Addison-Wesley.

————. 1973. *Husserl: Philosopher of Infinite Tasks.* Evanston: Northwestern University Press.

————. Ed. 1973. *Phenomenology and the Social Sciences.* Evanston: Northwestern University Press.

————. 1974. *Phenomenology, Role, and Reason: Essays on the Coherence and Deformation of Social Reality.* Springfield: Charles C. Thomas.

————. 1986. *Anonymity: A Study in the Philosophy of Alfred Schutz.* Bloomington: Indiana University Press.

Nghe, Nguyen. "Frantz Fanon et le probléme de l'indépendance." *La Pensée*, No. 107 (February 1963): 23–36.

Nietzsche, Friedrich. 1956. *"The Birth of Tragedy" and "The Genealogy of Morals."* Trans. by Francis Golffing. Garden City, New York: Doubleday and Company.

————. 1966. *Beyond Good and Evil: Prelude to a Philosophy of the Future.* Trans., with a commentary, by Walter Kaufmann. New York: Vintage Books.

————. 1968. *The Will to Power.* Trans. by Walter Kaufmann and R.J. Hollingdale. New York: Vintage Books.

Bibliography

Nisbet, Robert. 1973. *The Social Philosophers: Community and Conflict in Western Thought.* New York: Washington Square Press.

Onwuanibe, Richard C. *A Critique of Revolutionary Humanism: Frantz Fanon.* St. Louis, Missouri: Warren H. Green, 1983.

Parry, Benita. "Problem in Current Theories of Colonial Discourse." *Oxford Literary Review* 9, nos. 1–2 (1987): 27–58.

Parsons, Charles. 1967. "Foundations of Mathematics." *The Encyclopedia of Philosophy,* Vol. 5. New York: Macmillan & Free Press.

Prasad, Madhava. "The 'Other' Worldliness of Postcolonial Discourse: A Critique." *Critical Quarterly* 34, no. 3 (1992): 74–89.

Quine, W.V.O. 1969. *"Ontological Relativity" and Other Essays.* New York: Columbia University Press.

Robinson, Cedric. 1983. *Black Marxism: The Making of the Black Radical Tradition.* London: Zed Press.

———. "The Appropriation of Frantz Fanon." *Race & Class* 35, no. 1 (1993): 79–91.

Rosenau, Pauline Marie. 1992. *Post-Modernism and the Social Sciences: Insights, Inroads, and Intrusions.* Princeton: Princeton University Press.

Russell, Bertrand. 1912. *The Problems of Philosophy.* Oxford: Oxford University Press.

———. 1919. *Introduction to Mathematical Philosophy.* New York: Simon & Schuster.

Said, Edward. "Representing the Colonized: Anthropology's Interlocutors." *Critical Inquiry* 15, 2 (1989): 205–225.

Sappho. 1993. *Sappho: The Poems.* Revised Edition. Trans. by Sasha Newborn. Santa Barbara: Bandanna Books.

Sartre, Jean-Paul. 1943. *L'être et le néant: essai d'ontologie phénoménologique.* Paris: Gallimard.

———. 1955. In *"No Exit" and Three Other Plays.* New York: Vintage.

———. 1956. *Being and Nothingness: A Phenomenological Essay on Ontology.* Trans. with an intro. by Hazel E. Barnes. New York: Washington Square Press.

———. 1963. "Preface," In *The Wretched of the Earth.* New York: Grove Press, 1963. (See Fanon)

Bibliography

————. 1964, unpublished. *1964 Rome Lecture Notes*. Paris: Bibliothèque Nationale.

————. 1964. *The Words: The Autobiography of Jean-Paul Sartre*. Trans. by Bernard Frechtman. New York: George Braziller.

————.1968. *Search for a Method*. Trans. with an intro. by Hazel E. Barnes. New York: Vintage Books.

————. 1974. *Between Existentialism and Marxism: Sartre on Philosophy, Politics, Psychology, and the Arts*. Trans. by John Mathews. New York: Pantheon Books.

————. 1988. "Black Orpheus." In *"What Is Literature?" and Other Essays*. Trans. by John MacCombie. Ed. with an intro. by Steven Ungar. Cambridge, Mass.: Harvard University Press.

————. 1991. *Critique of Dialectical Reason*, Vol. I, *Theory of Practical Ensembles*. Trans. by Alan Sheridan-Smith and ed. by Jonathan Rée. London: Verso.

————. 1991. *Critique of Dialectical Reason*, Vol. II, *The Intelligibility of History*. Ed. by Arlette Elkaïm-Sartre and trans. by Quintin Hoare. London: Verso.

————. 1992. *Notebooks for an Ethics*. Trans. by David Pellauer with a foreword by Arlette Elkaïm-Sartre. Chicago: University of Chicago Press.

Schopenhauer, Arthur. 1883. *The World as Will and Idea*. Vol. I–III. Seventh Edition. Trans. by R.B. Haldane and J. Kemp. London: Kegan Paul, Trench, Trubner & Company.

Schrag, Calvin O. 1980. *Radical Reflection and the Origin of the Human Sciences*. West Lafayette, Indiana: Purdue University Press.

————. 1991. "Husserl's Legacy in the Postmodern World." *Analecta Husserliana* Vol. 30, 1991: 127–134.

————.1992. *The Resources of Rationality: A Response to the Postmodern Challenge*. Bloomington: Indiana University Press.

Schutz, Alfred. 1962. *Collected Papers*, Vol. I, *The Problem of Social Reality*. Ed. with an intro. by Maurice Natanson. Preface by H.L. Van Breda. Hague: Martinus Nijhoff.

————.1964. *Collected Papers*, Vol. II, *Studies in Social Theory*. Ed. with an intro. by Arvid Brodersen Hague: Martinus Nijhoff.

————.1966. *Collected Papers*, Vol. III, *Studies in Social Phenomenological Philosophy*. Ed. by Ilse Schutz. Hague: Martinus Nijhoff.

Bibliography

———.1967. *Phenomenology of the Social World.* Trans. by George Walsh and Frederick Lehnhert, with an intro. by George Walsh. Evanston: Northwestern University Press.

———.1970. *Reflections on the Problem of Relevance.* Ed. by Richard M. Zaner. New Haven, Connecticut: Yale University Press.

———.1973. *The Structures of the Life-World.* Trans. by Richard M. Zaner and H. Tristram Engelhardt, Jr. Evanston: Northwestern University Press, 1973.

———.1978. *The Theory of Social Action: The Correspondence of Alfred Schutz and Talcott Parsons.* Ed. by Richard Grathoff. Bloomington: Indiana University Press.

———.1989. *The Structures of the Life-World,* Vol. II. Trans. by Richard M. Zaner and David J. Parent. Evanston: Northwestern University Press.

Searle, John. 1991. "Response: Meaning, Intentionality, and Speech Acts." In *John Searle and His Critics.* Ed. by Lepore and Van Gulick. Oxford: Blackwell.

Sekyi-otu, Ato. Forthcoming. *Fanon's Dialectic of Experience.* Cambridge, Mass.: Harvard University Press.

Sophocles. 1954. *Sophocles I: "Oedipus the King," Trans. by David Grene, "Oedipus at Colonus," Trans. by Robert Fitzgerald, "Antigone," Trans. by Elizabeth Wyckoff.* Ed. with an Intro. by David Grene. Chicago: University of Chicago Press.

Sokolowski, Robert. 1974. *Husserlian Meditations: How Words Present Things.* Evanston: Northwestern University Press.

Sprinkler, Michael, ed. 1992. *Edward Said: A Critical Reader.* Oxford: Blackwell Publishers.

Taylor, Charles. 1979. *Hegel and Modern Society.* New York: Cambridge University Press.

Turner, Lou and John Alan. 1986. *Frantz Fanon, Soweto, and American Black Thought.* Chicago: News & Letters.

Walzer, Michael. 1988. *The Company of Critics: Social Criticism and Political Commitment in the Twentieth Century.* New York: Basic Books.

Weber, Max. 1922. *Wirtschaft und Gesellschaft.* Tübingen: Mohr.

———. 1946. *From Max Weber: Essays in Sociology.* Trans. and ed., with an intro. by H.H. Gerth and C. Wright Mills. New York: Oxford University Press.

Bibliography

————. 1966. *The Theory of Social and Economic Organization.* Trans. by A.M. Henderson and Talcott Parsons. Ed. with an intro. by Talcott Parsons. New York: The Free Press.

West, Cornel. 1994. *Keeping Faith: Philosophy and Race in America.* New York and London: Routledge.

Wilson, R. McL. 1967. "Mani and Manichaeism." In *The Encyclopedia of Philosophy,* Volume 5. New York: Macmillan and The Free Press.

Woddis, Jack. 1972. *New Theories of Revolution: A Commentary on the Views of Frantz Fanon, Régis Debray and Herbert Marcuse.* New York: International Publishers.

Zahar, Renate. 1970. *L'Oeuvre de Fantz Fanon.* Paris: Maspero.

————. 1974. *Frantz Fanon: Colonialism and Alienation, Concerning Frantz Fanon's Political Theory.* Trans. by Willfried F. Feuser. New York: Monthly Review Press.

Zolberg, Aristide, and Vera Zolberg. "The Americanization of Frantz Fanon." *Public Interest,* No. 9 (1966): 49–63.

Index

-A-

Abraham, 27, 45

Action, 8, 12, 29, 37, 47, 48, 50–52, 77

Active, 20

Adorno, Theodor, 43

Afracentric, 29

Africa, 28, 95–99

African American(s), 6, 93, 98. *See also* black Americans

African(s), 34, 93, 95–99

Afrocentricity, 18, 29

Agency, 45, 46, 47–50, 77

Ahmad, Aijaz, 100–101, 116

Alan, John, 116

Alexander "the Great", 63

Algeria, x, xii, 1, 6, 11, 34, 61, 64–66, 80–81, 94–96

Algerian woman, 34, 61, 63, 64

Algerian war of liberation, 1, 11, 64–65, 80–81, 96

Alienation, 21, 59, 93, 110

Alterity, 6, 43

Ambiguity, 21, 37

Americans, 28

American Indians, *See* Native Americans

Analytical philosophy, 51

Anderson, Marian, 42

Anguish, 44–45

Anonymity, 20, 37, 43, 47–48, 57–58, 61, 66, 76, 80, 87, 91, 111, 113

Anthropology, 2, 9, 11, 45, 80, 81

Antiblack racism, 24, 38, 30, 31

Antiblack world, 11–12, 25, 34

Antigone, The, 71, 74–75, 114

Antillean (French), 34

Antisemitism, 27, 43

Anti-Semite and Jew, 6, 27, 89

Anton, Antole, xi

Apartheid, 22

Apel, Karl Otto, 108

Apollo, 73

Arab(s), 11, 41, 41, 96–99

Arendt, Hannah, 68, 114

Aristotle, xiii, 15, 75, 67, 70, 73, 108, 112, 114

Index

Aron, Raymond, 46
Aronson, Ronald, 110
Austin, J.L., 112
Australian Aborigine, *See* Native
  Australian
Authenticity, 18, 25, 62
Asian, 28

–B–

Bad faith, 16–24, 29, 31, 34–35, 39,
  48–49, 62, 69, 87, 91, 110; and
  postcolonialism 111; racism, 24, 38;
  as a feature of crisis, 19, 23–24, 44,
  86, 90; institutional form, 21–24.
  See also Fanon, Gordon, Natanson,
  Sartre
Baltazar, Eulalio, 115
Barker, Francis, 107
Bastille, storming of the, 21
Beauvoir, Simone de, 45, 46, 109
Behnke, Elizabeth A, 18, 109
Being, 9, 10, 16–17
Being and Nothingness, 18, 19, 23, 89
Belief(s), 18, 52
Benjamin, Walter, 68
Bhabha, Homi, 88, 89, 90, 99, 100,
  101, 107, 111
Black(s), 11–12, 26, 28–29, 30, 34,
  46–47, 58–59, 75, 98–99, 115;
  "blackest," 99; body, 59–60; study
  of, 116; values, 31
Black American(s), 68–69, 93, 94
Black Jacobins, The, 82–83
Blackness, 24, 29, 32, 115; "fact of," 8,
  57
"Black Orpheus", 31, 32, 33, 39–40,
  110
Black philosophers, 14; of existence, 45
Black Skin, White Masks, 11, 68, 89
Black woman, 40, 106
Black Writers, Congress of, 95, 101
Blair, Robert, v, xiii

Blida-Joinville Hospital, 33, 95
Body, the, 19–20, 37, 45, 59, 63. *See
  also* embodiment
Bondage, *See* slavery
Boolean logic, 46
Bourgeoisie, 25–26, 90–91, 93–94;
  colonial, 8, 91; nationalist, 89; petit,
  90
Bracketing, 14, 15
*Brown versus Board of Education of Topeka
  Kansas*, 30
Buber, Martin, 43, 45
Buckley, R. Philip, 108
Bulhan, Hussein A., 2–3, 86, 94, 95, 99,
  113, 114, 115
Bywater, Ingram, 114

–C–

Cabral, Amilcar, 10
Canetti, Elias, 114
Capitalism, 90–91
Caribbean, 95, 98
Carnap, Rudolf, 43
Casey, Edward, 110
Cassinelli, C.W., 33, 109
Catharsis, 70, 71, 74, 102
Caucasians, 98
Caute, David, 14, 96, 99, 106
Central Intelligence Agency (CIA), 40
"Certain uncertainty", 59
Césaire, Aimé, 42, 96
China, 61
Choice, 22
Christianity, 26, 27, 28
"Civilized", 76; "white civilization," 7
Civil Rights Act of 1964, 30
Class oppression, 34, 90–91, 93, 111
Collective, 21, 22, 52–53
Colonialism, 6–11, 33–34, 38, 41, 42,
  60, 68, 69, 81, 87–101, 111
Colonized, the, 9–10, 32, 62, 65–66,
  77–83, 90, 99

130

Index

Colonizer, the, 77–83, 90
Consciousness, 15, 16, 19, 21, 32, 49.
    See Intentionality, Self,
    Transcendental
Constructivity, 47–54
Constitution (phenomenological problem of), 52
Contingency, 34
Creon, 71, 74
Crisis, xi, 7–12, 13, 19, 23–24, 25–26,
    37, 53–54, 86, 90, 102, 115; definition of, 12,   44, 86
Critical theory (philosophy), i, x,
    18–19, 35
Critical thought, 18
Critique of Dialectical Reason, 21, 89,
    110, 111
Crowd (ecstacy of), 74, 114
Crowell, Steven, 107
Cuba, xii, 95
Cultural critic, 2
Cultural criticism, 7, 61
Cultural studies (élite), 101
Culture, 24, 111

–D–
Davis, Horace, 113, 116
Death, 75–76
Debray, Régis, 68
Decolonization, 62, 70, 94
Deconstruction, 54, 111
Dehumanization, 11, 81
Depestre, René, 116
Descartes, René, 48
Desire, 10, 58
Dialectic(s), 14
Differentiation (acts of), 15
Dionysus, 73
Disembodiment, 20, 87
Domination, 11, 61
Dostoyevsky, Fyodor, 5, 105

Douglass, Frederick, 30–31, 67, 110,
    114
DuBois, W.E.B., 5, 10, 30, 106
Dummett, Michael, 112
Dying Colonialism, A, 32, 62–65

–E–
Edie, James, 107
Ego, 8, 49. See also Transcendental
Egoism, 72–74
Eidetic reduction, 15
Ellison, Ralph, 5, 106
Embodiment, 19–21, 58–60
Enemy, the, 80–81
Equalizing matters, 76
Epistemic clarity, 15–16
Epistemology, 43, 57, 99
Essence, 15, 46, 51, 53–57
Europe, 6, 12, 28; European, 65, 81
European Man (European Humanity),
    6–9, 26, 27, 35, 60–61, 102–103
European philosophers, 46
European scientists, 3
Euro-Reason, 6
Euripides, 73
Everyday, the, 39, 41–42, 58, 62, 66,
    110; liberating transformation of,
    42
Evidence, 17, 23, 29
Existence, 10, 14, 35, 37, 45, 71–72;
    philosopher of, 43–45, 93
Existentialism, 24, 44, 92–93
Existential phenomenology, xi, 10,
    14–24, 35, 43, 44–46, 69–70, 113
Existential philosophers, 45
Explanation, 39–41, 47
Extension, 51
Exteriority, 31

–F–
Facticity, 30, 31, 38, 110
Faith, 27

Familiarity, 17, 38

Fanon and the Psychology of Oppression, 2

Fanon, Frantz, v, ix–xii, 1–3, 5–12, 14, 17, 19, 24–28, 33–35, 38, 40–43, 45–47, 50–51, 52, 57, 59–66, 68–71, 75, 77–81, 83, 86–103, 106, 108, 116; and postcolonialism, 87–102, 110; as critique of European/Western society, chap. 1; Caribbean expatriate, 95–96; "European interloper," 98; tragic writer, 83, chap. 4; attitude toward peasants, 89; birth and death of, 1; humor, 89; Fanonian phenomenology, 45–46, 113; monuments to, 86, 94–95; on anonymity, 42, 57; bad faith, 35; blaming victims, 40; colonialism, 40, 61, 70, 77; decolonization, 70; embodiment, 59–60; everyday, the, 57, 62; history, 24–26, 32–35; human sciences, 50–51; ontology, 9–10, 17, 24, 28; power, 25; racism, 38, 60; racist explanations, 40; revolutionary praxis, 62–66; Sartrism, 21; violence, 68–71, 77–78, 80–81, 83, 115; speaking to Arab patients, 96–97; humor of, 92, 115; parents of, 95, 116; resignation from Blida-Joinville, 33–34; right-wing efforts to assassinate, 96

Federal Bureau of Investigations (FBI), 40

Figes, Eva, 63, 67, 70, 71, 74, 113

Flesh, 19–20

Foucault, Michel, 101

Fourteenth Amendment, 30

France, 6, 11, 61

Freedom, 11, 16–17, 37, 67, 69, 89; "in the flesh," 11, 19, 50

Free variation, 15

Frege, Gottlob, 51, 112

Freire, Paulo, 62, 113, 114

Freud, Sigmund, 71, 99, 114

Front de Liberation Nationale (FLN), 1, 34, 62–65

–G–

Gates, Jr., Henry Louis, 87–89, 90, 91, 94–95, 99–102, 106, 107

Gays, 75

Geismar, Peter, 99, 106

Genocide, 22

Global Theory, 87, 88, 99, 90

God, 8, 20, 76

Good faith, 18

Gooding-Williams, Robert, 116

Goldberg, David Theo, 107, 112

Gordon, Lewis R., 105, 107, 109, 111, 116

Grene, David, 114

Guevera, Che, 68

Gutman, Herbert G., 111

–H–

Habermas, Jürgen, 7, 106

Haiti, 66, 82

Hansen, Emmanuel, 1–2, 95, 98, 99, , 105, 114, 115

Hare, Nathan, 106

Harris, Leonard, x, xi, 107, 115

Hegel, G.W.F., 2, 21, 93, 110; on history, 28–29; tragedy, 71, 72, 114

Heidegger, Martin, 45, 53

Henry, Paget, ix

Historicism, 25

History, 20, 23–33, 100, 110; Hegelian, 28–29; histories, 28; Natansonian, 29. *See* Fanon

Hitler, Adolf, 26, 33

Holocaust, 43

Hontoundji, Pauline, 47, 111

Howells, Christina, 110

Human being(s), 17, 23, 46, 54, 80

Index

Humanism, 10–12, 32, 35, 43, 69–70
Humanity, 8, 12, 20, 22, 25, 31, 86–87
Human nature, 35, 87
Human reality, 17, 45, 53
Human science(s), 2–3, 13, 35, 50–51, 87, 99, 103
Husserl, Edmund, 2, 6–8, 17, 25, 26, 43, 46, 52, 53, 103, 107, 108, 109, 112; conception of phenomenology, 14–17; on crisis, 7–8; European humanity, 6; philosophy, 103

–I–
Ideal, 9. *See also* type(s), typification
Ideology, 2, 22, 24
Illych, Ivan, 58
Indians, 28
India, 61
Individual, 19, 29, 49–50
Individualism, 43
Indonesia, 66
Intellectual, 8, 46
Intension, 51, 107
Intentionality, 15, 51–52
Intentions, 107
Interiority, 31, 58
Invisibility, 38
Invisible, 17, 38

–J–
James, C.L.R. , 20, 82–83, 91, 115
James, Joy, xii
Jameson, Fredric, 69, 109, 110, 111
JanMohamed, Abdul, 88, 89, 90
Jazz, 21–22
Jeanson, Francis, 46
Jesus of Nazareth, 26, 78
Jews, 26, 27–28, 75
Jinadu, L. Adele, 99, 111, 113, 114, 115, 116
Jocasta, 75
Jones, William R., 76, 78–79, 115

Judgment(s), 15
Justice, 25–26, 34, 75, 77, 81; racial, 25–26

–K–
Kant, Immanuel, 27, 45, 99
Kierkegaard, Sfren, 27, 43, 45
King, Jr., Martin Luther, 76, 78–79
King, Rodney, 102
Knowledge, 18

–L–
Lacan, Jacques, 101, 107
Lamumba, Patrice, v
Language, 35, 48, 51, 52, 96–97; theriomorphic, 60; zoological, 60
Lattimore, Richard, 114
Legitimation, 7, 22, 63–64
Lenin, Vladimir, 12
Lévi-Strauss, Claude, 101
Liberalism, xi
Liberation, 29, 32, 43, 81, 92; discourse 100, 101
Liberation theory, ix, 42–43, 71, 90, 92, 100, 101
Libertarianism, 93
Liberty, 69, 89
Life, 20, 49, 72
Life-world, 16, 25, 38, 72
Literary theory, 102–103
Local narratives, 61
Locke, Alain, 13, 37, 107, 109–110, 111
Lott, Tommy, xi, 109
Lukács, George, 43
Lyotard, Jean-François, 43, 87, 115

–M–
Madness, 11
Malraux, André, 96
Man, 9–12, 33
Manichaeanism, 8, 33
Mannoni, Dominique, 113

Index

Mao Tse Tung, 33, 68, 79
Marcuse, Herbert, x, 43
Martinique, 1, 86, 94, 96, 98
Marx, Karl, 21, 109, 115
Marxism, 24, 61, 89, 92, 92–94, 109, 111
Masochism, 19, 20, 22–23
Master, the, 34, 80
Matustík, Martin, x, xi, 105
McBride, William L., 111
Meaning, 16, 51–53
Mediation, 15, 31, 69, 70
Medicine, 65
Memmi, Albert, 88, 94, 99, 106
Merleau-Ponty, Maurice, 13, 14, 15, 17, 19, 46, 106, 108, 112, 113; critique of Mill, 113; on anonymity of the body, 37
Metaphysical guilt, 35
Method, 25, 45
Methodology, 9
Mill, John Stuart, 112, 113
Mind, philosophy of, 51–52
Misanthropy, 20; misanthropic times, x
Moral duty, 27
Mundanity, 29, 38, 42–43, 107
Muslim(s), 75
Myth-making, 2

–N–

Natanson, Maurice, xiii, 38, 43, 49–50, 57–58, 107, 110, 112, 113; on micro history, 29
Native American, 28, 61
Native Australian, 28
Natural attitude, 15
Natural sciences, 48, 51, 100
Nazis, 26, 27
Negativity, 17
Negritude, 31–33, 95, 110, 113
Neocolonialism, 6, 69, 79, 87–101, 111
Newton, Huey, 68

Nghe, Nguyen, 92
Nietzsche, Friedrich, 8, 35, 68, 71, 73–74, 80
Nihilism, 24, 43, 72
Nonviolence, 77–79
Normality, 26, 38, 47, 57, 62
North Africans, 98–99

–O–

Objectivity, 9, 31, 37, 53, 59, 75
Occupation, the, 43, 61
Oedipus, 63, 75, 114
Ontogeny, 9
Ontology, 9–10, 15, 17, 24, 28, 35, 43, 46, 49, 50
Onwuanibe, Richard, 95, 116
Oppressed, the, 25, 32, 75, 99
Oppression, 41–43, 62, 87, 88
Ordinary (the), 17, 41; names, 56
"Orientals", 28
Other, the, 6, 11, 19–20, 23, 43, 49
Other selves (problem of), 48–49
Overdetermination, 6, 30, 58, 59, 76

–P–

Parry, Benita, 88, 89, 90, 106
Parsons, Charles, 112
Passive, 20
Pathos, 70
Pegasus, 51
People of color, 7, 27–28, 68, 75, 100, 115
Perception, 15, 20, 24–25
Perspectivity, 19
Pessimism, 72
Phallus, 107
Phenomenologist, 16
Phenomenology, 14–18, 29, 35, 37–39, 45, 53–54, 56, 60, 63, 111, 113
Philosophy, 12, 13, 23–24, 103; of existence, 24, 43–45, 109 political, 2. *See also* black philosophers, critical

Index

theory (philosophy), European philosophers, existential philosophy

Phylogeny, 9

Physicalism, 48

Physicians, 33–34, 65, 96–97

Pierce, Charles Sanders,

"Place", 32, 110

Plato, 26

Pogroms, 22

Police brutality, 102

Political, the, 71

Political science, 102

Popper, Sir Karl, 51, 112

Positivism, 51

Postcolonialism, 62, 69, 87–101, 111

Postmodern, 44, 88, 89, 91, 97, 111, 113

Poststructuralism, 6, 35, 88, 89, 100, 107, 111, 113

Poussaint, Alvin, 106

Poverty, 39

Power, 25, 63, 79, 87

Powerful, the, 25, 73, 75

Powerless, the, 25, 75

Practico-inert, 22, 34

Prague, xi–xii

Praxis, 10, 15, 32, 35, 62–66, 86, 93, 101

Présence Africaine, 95

Present, the (domination of), 23

"Pressure of prejudice", 17–81

Progress, 31, 32, 101, 110

Progressive-regressive, 75

Proletariat, 25, 31, 33, 93

Proper names, 56

Psychological, the, 71, 92

Psychology, 3, 13, 15, 21, 92

Psychoanalysis, 7, 63, 71, 99, 107, 113

–Q–

Questioner, 16

Questioning, 16, 25

Quine, Willard V. O., 51, 112

–R–

Race, 24, 28, 41, 46, 47, 51; and the urban, 102

Racial discrimination, 30

Racism, 6, 11, 25–26, 30, 38, 39, 42, 47, 60, 68, 98, 116; and pathology, 40–41; invisibility of, 38; post-, 80

Radicality, 10, 16, 54, 87, 94, 101, 103, 108

Rape, 40, 63, 77

Rationality, 7–9, 73

Reason, 6–8, 24, 27

Recognition, 22–23, 29; human, 22

Reading Rodney King, 102, 116

Reduction (phenomenological), 15–16

Reductionism, 116

Referent, 51

Reflection, 15, 39, 47

Relevance (problem of), 56, 94, 102–103

Resignation, 11, 72

Resistance-fighter, 80

Responsibility, 17, 24, 75

"Reverse discrimination", 25, 77

Revolution, 25, 31, 32–33, 52, 62, 65, 66, 89, 90–91, 93

"Revolutionary War" (US), 30

Rights of Man, 27

Rigor, 10, 54

Robinson, Cedric, 89–90, 91–94, 101, 102, 106, 115

Rorty, Richard, 7

Rousseau, Jean-Jacques, xiii, 21, 80

Russell, Bertrand, 112

Rwanda, 66

–S–

Sadism, 19–20, 22–23, 61

Said, Edward, 88, 89, 90, 100, 115

Salvation, 25–27

135

Sappho, 85, 115
Sartre, ix, 6, 14–27, 42, 43, 45, 46, 48,
75, 89, 106, 109, 110, 111, 113;
existential phenomenology of,
14–24; on bad faith, 17–18; bour-
geoisie, the, 90–91; class struggle,
34; History, 31, 32, 33; negritude,
31–33
Scape goat, 74
Schopenhauer, Arthur, 71, 72
Schrag, Calvin O., 20, 37, 108, 115
Schutz, Alfred, 17, 37, 38, 43, 47, 52,
107, 108, 111, 112, 113; on social
reality, 17, 50
Science, 3, 14
Searle, John, 51–53, 112
Self, 11; -consciousness, 2, 28–29;
recovery, 18
Senghor, Léopold S., 31, 95
Seriality, 22, 34
Sincerity, 18
Situation, 31, 45
Slave (the), 10, 11, 23, 26, 30–31, 41;
former, 69
Slavery, 22, 28, 40, 67, 111
"Social construction", 47–48, 50
Sociality (social reality), 17, 20–22, 45,
53, 59, 87
Socialism, 24
Social role, 31
Social science(s), 2, 47, 52–53, 112
Social theory, 46, 55, 90
Sociogenesis, 9, 34, 45
Society, 34
Socrates, 73
Sophocles, 71
Sokolowski, Robert, 107, 112
South America, 28
Spirit of seriousness, 22, 29, 33, 47
Spivak, Gayatri, 88, 89, 90, 101
Stalin, J.V., 33
Stereotyping, 56

Stone, Robert, x
Subjectivity, 9, 19, 37, 58, 77; inter-, 50
Substance(s), 15, 53

–T–
Taylor, Charles, 110
Technology, 64–65
Texts, 61, 102–103
Textuality, 102–103, 116
Theory, 90, 91, 102–103
"They," the, 57
Third World, the, 90
Thirteenth Amendment, 30
Thou-orientation, 49
Token(s), 54–55
Tolstoi, Leo, 58
Torturers, 80
Tragedy, 63, 67, 70, 75, 80–83, 114
Tragos, 74
Transcendental, 16, 21, 49, 107; argu-
ment 21; ego, 16; experience, 16;
subject, 15, 45
Truth, 23
Truth, Sojourner, 45
Tucker, Robert, 109
Turner Lou, 116
Type(s), 54–56; ideal, 55
Typify, 17
Typification, 17, 54–56
Tyrannus, 14

–U–
Underclass, 33, 89
Urban, 41
United States, 1, 6, 30, 66, 97, 102

–V–
Validity, 10, 100
Value(s), 8, 13, 21–25, 31, 33, 35, 37,
38, 41, 54, 101–102
Venus (planet), 51
Victimization, 76

Viet Nam War, 78
Violence, 41, 68, 70, 71, 76–83; black-on-black, 41; white-on-white, 41
Visible, 17
Visibility, 17–19
"Voice of Algeria, the", 65

–W–
Wahl, Jean, 46
Walzer, Michael, 113
Weber, Max, 48, 50, 52, 55, 112, 113
West, Cornel, 113
Western man, 8, 35
West Indians, 99
"We" relationships, 49
White(s), 11, 25–26, 41, 46, 60–61, 98
White man, 8, 10, 11, 12, 34, 106
Whiteness, 33; as normative, 11–12, 25
White problem, 27
White Renée, 116
White supremacist(s), 25–26

White woman, 8
Wittgenstein, Ludwig, 48
Woddis, Jack, 92, 113, 116
Women, 75. *See also* Algerian women, black women, white women
Wonder, Stevie,
Working-class, 24, 33, 39, 89, 93
World, 15, 16; end of, 11
Wretched of the Earth, The, 68, 70, 83, 89, 90–91

–X–
X, Malcolm (El-Haji Malik El-Shabazz), v, 30, 68, 78–79

–Y–
Yugoslavia (former), 66

–Z–
Zahar, Renate, 93, 99, 110, 116